Mother Was a Rebel

Also by Helen Blackshear

Southern Smorgasbord

The Creek Captives

Alabama Album

From Peddlar to Philanthropist

These I Would Keep

Silver Songs

Vanished in the Unknown Shade

MOTHER WAS A REBEL

Tuscaloosa Sketches "... in praise of gentle people"

Helen F. Blackshear

NewSouth Books
Montgomery | Louisville

NewSouth Books
P.O. Box 1588
Montgomery, AL 36102

Copyright © 2007 by Helen F. Blackshear
All rights reserved under International and Pan-American Copyright Conventions. Published in the United States by NewSouth Books, a division of NewSouth, Inc., Montgomery, Alabama.

Library of Congress Cataloging-in-Publication Data

ISBN-13: 978-1-60306-037-0
ISBN-10: 1-60306-037-5

Publication History
A slightly different version of this book was privately published by the author in 1973 and was reprinted in 1976. In addition, three of the sketches, "Grandmother Linka's House," "Uncle Bob and the Rain Song," and "Mama Sayre" had been previously published in the *Georgia Review*.

Design by Randall Williams
Printed in the United States of America

TO MY DAUGHTERS
ANNE, SUE, AND LEN

"Say, is there Beauty yet to find?

And Certainty? and Quiet kind?"

— Rupert Brooke

Contents

Mother Was a Rebel / 9

Grandmother Linka's House / 18

Uncle Bob and the Rain Song / 26

Steamboat Whistle / 38

Mammy Was Not a Myth / 46

Our Homemade Automobile / 57

Grandmother Longshore / 62

Out Reluctant Suitors / 73

Seasoned Lightly with "Alabama Corn" / 88

College Days—A World Without Boys / 97

They Called Him Singing Sam / 115

Uncle Hugo and the Crimson Tide / 126

Dreamhouse for a Dollar a Day / 147

New York on Fifteen Dollars a Week / 153

Mary Bacon / 169

Mama Sayre, Scott Fitzgerald's Mother-in-Law / 185

"Aunt Mary" / 195

Rebel to the End / 200

Chapter 1

Mother Was a Rebel

My mother was not particularly fond of children, so she usually found a way to spend as little time as possible with my small brother and me. Fortunately for us, we had Mammy, who lived upstairs. She was the one who actually raised us. One of my earliest recollections is of being picked up in Mammy's strong yellow arms and carried inside from the icy sleeping porch. Mother was a firm believer in fresh air for children. However, it was Mammy who carried us out of the frigid air to sit on her ample lap front of the glowing coal fire in her bedroom where she would bathe, dress and feed us. She also attended to our manners and morals with kindly patience, and refereed our battles, which were constant and ferocious. Then, at night, Mammy listened to our prayers, rocked us to sleep, and put us to bed at the first sign of darkness. As our parents customarily spent their evenings at bridge or the movies, we rarely saw them before breakfast time.

Mother must have got her odd ideas about child care from reading English novels that were full of nannies and nurseries. We children were fed separately in the breakfast room. Not until we were considered old enough to eat with proper manners were we allowed in the dining room at night to eat with our parents.

Mother's own Longshore upbringing had been very different. She was the fourth of twelve children. Her father was a small-town probate judge. She had been accustomed to a long table loaded with homegrown foods which her mother had labored for hours to prepare in her steaming kitchen. When Mother was twenty years old and had graduated from Judson, a sedate female Baptist institute, she met and married a well-to-do, sophisticated bachelor of forty, stubbornly turned her back on country ways, devoting the rest of her life to becoming a woman of the world. Although she never quite succeeded, it was not for lack of trying. At her wedding, she announced to the assembled Longshores that she would never again be "Annie Laurie" and *particularly* not "Annie." She would be known as Laurie! That was her declaration of independence.

When I was a small child I often resented my mother's youthful good looks and the many and varied activities that kept her so busy. On the other hand, I adored my quiet grandmother, and spent much time at my friend Mary's house, where *her* mother, "Miss Abbie" Rau, would usually be working in the kitchen or at her sewing machine or such other places as I judged it was proper for mothers to be. Looking back, I can see that I must have been a most unsatisfactory child because I was sulky and willful.

I was thankful that, as an experiment, Mother had taught me to read when I was quite young. Books were my constant refuge and sometimes even Mary, whom I loved dearly, could not persuade me to come down from my perch in the mulberry tree, where I would retreat with one of my favorites. My mother and I were opposites and thus often adversaries but we did have respect for one another. It was not until many years later that I understood her somewhat better, although even then no confidences were shared between us.

The principal reason for Mother's having become Grandmother Longshore's "only ungrateful child" was her friend, Helen Leeper.

The Leepers were a well-traveled family, their manners and tastes had been refined by experience, and their house was the only one in the entire town at that time that boasted running water and electric lights. Consequently, they were a group apart and much envied by others. They were often called snobbish, and it was even rumored that Mr. Leeper "drank." However, to Annie Laurie, whose strict Baptist parents considered even innocent card-playing a sin and whose home contained not the faintest trace of luxury, the carefree gaiety of the Leepers was most exhilarating. The friendship with Helen Leeper continued even after my mother's marriage, indeed throughout their entire lives. I was named for Mother's friend and was taught to call her "Aunt Helen."

One of the things about the Leepers that was a particular shock to the Longshores was that they seldom attended church. The simple reason was that they were Episcopalians and the only churches in town were the Baptist and Methodist.

Annie Laurie's first major rebellion was against the church when she was about eighteen. It was customary in those days for courting couples of Columbiana to drive their buggies over to Shelby Springs for amusement. That was a "watering place" whose hotel, pavilion and sulphur springs were widely known. These jaunts were not frowned upon until word got around that dancing was going on in the pavilion. This caused an uproar and tempers flared.

One fateful Sunday, the Baptist preacher announced from the pulpit the names of some young people whom the congregation had decided to reprimand for going dancing. Young Annie Laurie stood up angrily in her place and called out, "I've been to Shelby Springs with the others, and I didn't dance because my parents disapproved. But if you're going to put them out of the church, you can just as well put me out, too!" That was the last time my mother ever went to church!

Years later, she told me that about the same time as the church incident she happened to read in a newspaper that the governor was giving a ball. The twin gods of her household had always been politics and religion, so surely, if the governor invited people to dance, it couldn't be so wrong. Following that reasoning a few months later, she accepted an invitation from her first cousin, Jack Persons, to the commencement dance at the University of Alabama in Tuscaloosa where she met my father and fell in love immediately! She allowed him to sign for most of the dances on her card, to the chagrin of Cousin Jack, who had spent much time lining up prospective partners for his country cousin.

Mother told me that my daddy was so very handsome and such an excellent dancer that she didn't pay the slightest attention to Jack's warning that he had already reached his fortieth birthday and was a confirmed bachelor!

Actually, my parents' marriage was looked on with disapproval by almost everybody except the two of them. The Longshores, I suspect, would only have found a Catholic less acceptable as a son-in-law than a Jew. However, Daddy had been brought up among Christians and had never even seen the inside of a synagogue. Many years later, his warm and lovable nature had finally won them all over. As for my father's family, they mistrusted my mother's youth and lack of social experience. Daddy's young stepmother, Linka, and his older sister, Emma, never truly accepted my mother as a member of their family. Although no word of criticism was ever voiced in my presence, and I spent every Sunday with Grandmother Linka and frequently visited Aunt Emma in Gadsden, I cannot recall any visits of either of those ladies to our home.

I grew up in the age of Victorian formality. Ladies paid afternoon calls wearing white gloves and top-heavy, over-trimmed hats. They swapped recipes for elaborate desserts and exchanged complicated crochet patterns. They spent vacations on sedate sightseeing tours or at the same stodgy summer hotels. My father's friends must have done their best to welcome his young bride and tried to include her in their invitations, but Mother never felt truly at ease among those women, twenty years older than she was. Their conversation centered on servant problems and children, and she was bored to death, as she put it, at their ice-cream-and-cake parties.

For a few years, she did her level best to fit into that unfamiliar world. Not long ago I found a packet of sad little letters written to Daddy from the beach resort to which Mother had been temporarily exiled with her two little ones. She said she was very lonely and was sure that he was enjoying his poker games and his friends and didn't miss her at all. That mood of self-pity was very unlike her and fortunately didn't last long. Her boundless energy and her eagerness to learn new things gradually made her one of the leaders of the group of younger women whose ideas were soon to revolutionize the entire social setup of our quiet, old-fashioned town.

Sarah Moody, who was one of Mother's lifelong friends, recently gave me a letter written in 1911, just a year after Mother's marriage, in which Mother welcomed Sarah to Tuscaloosa. "There are so few young married people here," she had written, "and some way I have felt that we would be friends. I have told Sam so often this winter that I hoped you and Frank would marry. I am one year ahead of you. Still I think we might be rather congenial."

One thing that may have promoted the congeniality between them was that Frank, like my daddy, was a good deal older than his wife. There was also the attraction of their mutual interest in new ideas such as votes for women, an idea that rather startled my father. They also had in common an intense love of books, an interest in the theater and in stimulating conversation. Sarah, who had been an art teacher, was an intelligent and charming person. There were other younger women in the group as well. I particularly remember a vivacious redhead, Nell Clarkson, who had a hearty laugh; friendly and serene Ira Moody, and tall dark-haired

Mary Bacon Clabaugh with her husky voice and sparkling wit. Those friends would often meet at each other's homes for lunch, an informal entertainment which gradually took the place of the "sticky" ice cream parties. By the time I was old enough for school, Mother and Daddy had dropped out of the Tuesday Night Bridge Club, in which a dozen sedate couples played auction bridge, and at which Mother had become known not for her bridge prowess but for her Delmonico pudding liberally laced with brandy.

Mother's own group formed a new kind of club which resolutely turned its face to the present under the name "Up to Date Club," its goal to keep abreast of the times. That club expressed my mother's philosophy more than any of the other activities she engaged in. Each member was assigned to research and then present a paper on some concern of modern life. This led to Mother's absorbing herself completely for months at a time in such studies as Russian drama and Mexican folk art at the university library.

While I was growing up, I recall being taken to music recitals and lectures given by visiting celebrities and I still have a vivid recollection of a hilarious but somehow pathetic spectacle of the poet Vachel Lindsay, with his long arms and ungainly figure, leading the audience in chanting, 'Are you washed in the blood of the Lamb?" or "Then I saw the Congo creeping through the black/ Cutting through the jungle with a golden track . . ." Afterwards, Mother invited him to an impromptu party at our home, where he repeated the performance from atop our grand piano.

Some of Mother's enthusiasm for culture had originated during their European honeymoon tour in the summer of 1910. For several months at one time she tried to teach conversational French to my brother and me by making us speak it at mealtimes. Either we were not too bright or her patience was too short, for the experiment was a total failure. Her own efforts lasted somewhat longer and included auditing a French course at the university with her friend, Jean

Moody. I recall coming into the living room once to find Mother and Jean sitting cross-legged on the rug playing "Memory" with French vocabulary words written on scraps of paper.

"Aunt Jean" had a lovely smile and a great zest for life. She was a favorite with me. She had been a school friend of Mother's and had met Max, her doctor husband, while she was visiting our house. Max was our family doctor, taking care of all of us during our bouts with measles or whooping cough. I always associate his gentle, reassuring voice with the stacks of old *National Geographic*s that Daddy brought home from his office on those rare occasions when I was sick in bed. As for Mother, she was always in vigorous health. I don't remember her requiring Max's services except when my two younger sisters were born.

Perhaps one reason for Mother's exceptional health was her love of golf. She and Daddy had learned to play the game in Scotland, and their eagerness to continue led to the building of Tuscaloosa's first golf course. Down the hill behind our Pinehurst home was a strip of woodland and, beyond that, rolling meadows bordered the river. One Sunday afternoon when I was very small I watched while Daddy, who was a civil engineer, with sweeping gestures, showed Mother the clumps of wild Cherokee roses that would be removed to make way for future greens and fairways. In due time, the course was completed, but there was nobody for Mother to play golf with except Daddy. Over the years her enthusiasm was so contagious that she taught the new game to several of her friends, and when the country club was eventually built, it became one of the absorbing interests of her life.

In those days, housekeeping did not present many problems as help was plentiful. We had a laundress, a yardman, and a cook who prepared breakfast and the evening meal. Sometimes a woman would come in to sew, a chore which Mother detested. However, she did have a gift for flower arrangements. Our yard was filled with roses, camellias, azaleas and irises against a background of climbing roses and trailing wisteria vines. The vases of the downstairs rooms were always aglow with color, from the earliest flowering quince of February through the roses and larkspur of summer, the red and gold leaves and chrysanthemums of autumn, to the spicy cedar sprays and holly of Christmas. Mother could not abide artificial wax flowers or dried blossoms. At Christmas time we always had a family outing to select the finest cedar tree and holly berries from Daddy's own woodlands to decorate the house.

Mother's principal innovations in the domestic field were in the realm of food. She remained loyal to the turnip greens and cornbread remembered from her childhood, although we children disliked them, and she refused to serve most of the rich pastries and starchy dishes that were then in vogue. She even went so far as to take a course at the university in nutrition. My poor daddy could rarely persuade her to serve his beloved sauerkraut and boiled potatoes or the thick goulashes that his Hungarian family served. Her tastes ran to fresh garden vegetables, crisp salads, meats in their natural juices, and light desserts. There were few times, and those were probably birthdays, when we were allowed cake with icing. However, for special events, Mother's prize recipe was a twelve-egg almond cake, the batter consisting almost entirely of ground almonds. She tried, with mixed success, to win our approval for her broccoli Hollandaise, artichokes with lemon-butter sauce and avocado pears. Only when I went to visit my Grandmother Linka on Sundays did I ever get the golden fried chicken and gooey chocolate concoctions that I loved so much.

Whatever guidance was lacking due to my relations with my mother, whose tastes ran counter to the domestic, was made up for by Daddy's gentle stepmother, whom I dearly loved. With the contrariness of a willful child, which I was, I became enamored of the very qualities against which Mother had rebelled—the unchanging routine, the massive house and its heavy furnishings, the rich cuisine and, above all, the ever-present romance of the past.

Chapter Two

Grandmother Linka's House

When I was four years old I ran away from home. It was a bright Spring morning when I took off, leaving my frantic mother and half the neighborhood to search and worry. I wasn't in the least bit lost. I had simply decided to walk the mile across town to my Grandmother Linka's house to pick violets. There were hundreds lining the geometric-patterned walks in the gardens that surrounded her big white-columned house. The previous Sunday when I had been taken there for a visit, Grandmother had remarked that the violets needed picking and that, for each that was picked, two new ones would grow in its place. She had knelt down to show me exactly how to break them carefully at the base of the stem so as not to snap off their heads. I kept at it until I had a great big bunch as a surprise for my grandmother. And she was indeed surprised, especially when she found that I had run away from home to pick them.

    I don't recall ever being punished by my gentle grandmother, although she made me understand that it was thoughtless of me to frighten folks so. On that occasion, she spoke to me in a firm, serious voice just as if I were grown up. Then, I was taken in to wash my grubby hands and given a bowl of strawberries in the outdoor kitchen that was always full of good smells.

A few years later, a modern kitchen was installed, but when I was small, Grandmother used the outside kitchen where her gleaming black coal range stood on a gray marble hearth in the middle of the room. There were rows of preserves on the open shelves and a bag of cream cheese usually hung by the door to drip. At meal times, Grandmother had to carry the hot food across the brick courtyard in large covered dishes to the *rathskeller*, which was what she and Uncle Hugo called their basement dining room. She was partly sheltered on rainy days by a wooden bridge that crossed from the upstairs porch to the rooms above the outside kitchen that had once belonged to the house slaves.

I adored the *rathskeller* with its dark panelled walls, beautiful bentwood chairs and row of beer steins lined up on a shelf too high for me to reach. But I loved Grandmother's cooking even more. It was not merely a skill with her; it was an art! She collected hundreds of recipes but knew hundreds more by heart. After her death, we found notebooks full of them written in her spidery boarding-school script, from old German dishes handed down in her family to elaborate recipes for party desserts she had collected from her friends and from ladies' magazines. During all of my childhood years, Grandmother's Sunday dinners were the highlight in my week.

Sometimes my bachelor Uncle Hugo, who was quite a hunter, would provide partridge or wild duck, but my favorite meal was fried chicken, dipped in egg batter and bread crumbs, and for dessert her caramel custard ice cream or chocolate icebox cake, which contained marshmallows, pecans, maraschino cherries and other glazed fruits in a rich fudge batter with ladyfingers surrounding the whole thing. I still don't know how my grandmother kept her tiny, graceful figure.

After those delectable dinners, as might be expected, Grandmother and Uncle Hugo would often take a nap or she would take up her crocheting and rock in her low padded armchair. Grandmother also collected crochet and embroidery patterns and the more difficult ones could keep her happily absorbed for hours. I don't think there was a piece of linen in that house that didn't boast a border or monogram of her dainty stitching. This pastime of Grandmother's left me free to enjoy my other great love—her wonderful house. Sometimes I would read, but as there were few books in the glass-doored bookcases of interest to a child, after I had sampled *Gulliver's Travels* or *Tanglewood Tales* for the third or fourth time, I amused myself by wandering through the huge front parlors.

Although that mansion, formerly called the Battle House, had been built in the 1830s, my grandfather didn't buy it until after the Civil War, when its former owners moved up North. The furniture, therefore, belonged to the elaborate late Victorian period—vases and bric-a-brac were everywhere, many of the pieces hand-painted Limoges. There were gilt-framed portraits and landscapes on the walls and richly carved, uncomfortable "lady" and "gentleman" chairs and loveseats. In one room was a great square rosewood piano which I could sometimes persuade Grandmother to play, but best of all were the floor to ceiling pier mirrors and the magnificent tiered crystal chandeliers. Those and the handmade lace curtains had been purchased in Europe by my long-dead grandfather as a gift for his first bride. I heard a cousin say that the lace had been made by Grandfather's relatives in Hungary, from which country he had come to America in the 1850s. Those curtains were my Grandmother Linka's greatest treasures. The fragile lace is falling to pieces now as they have been mended beyond repair, but to me they are still beautiful.

Grandmother and Uncle Hugo rarely used the two big front parlors, preferring to sit in the sunny corner of the formal dining room which stretched along the rear of the first floor. In the pantry off the near end was a contrivance that fascinated me when I was a child, although I never saw it actually being used. It was a large dumbwaiter on which food from the outdoor kitchen used to be placed and hauled up by rope pulleys. The little pantry with its rows of unused china was close and dusty, but I liked to imagine the old days when Grandmother was young and held the big dinner parties which were in vogue in those days. But it was the front parlors with their high, frescoed ceilings that were most exciting as they had so many "Don't touch" things. A marble statue of Venus stood on the center table, but my special favorite was a statue of a little curly-haired girl reading forever as she sat in her marble chair at the base of the tallest mirror. The inscription in her book was in Latin and I resolved every Sunday that some day I'd learn what it said.

In those quiet parlors or on the sandy garden walks or under the magnolia trees, I would imagine playing games with the little girl who had once lived in that house with her uncle long before the Civil War. Her name had been Virginia and they told me that she had grown up to be a great beauty and had married a famous senator named Clement C. Clay.

In her autobiography, *Belle of the Fifties*, Virginia Clay-Clopton wrote: "My recollections of that early Alabama life center about a great house set in widening grounds in the midst of which was a wondrous magnolia tree white with bloom . . . Around that tree we played 'Chickamy, Chickamy, Craney Crow' and, at the climax, 'What o'clock, Old Witch?,' would scamper wildly to elude the pursuit of the imaginary witch. Here, a healthy and happy child, I pursued my studies. Association with my uncle, Thomas B. Tunstall, Secretary of State of Alabama, fed the finer side of my nature and inspired in me the love of things literary even at an age when I had hardly handled a book. My memory crowds with pictures of my Uncle Tom walking slowly up and down, playing his violin and interspersing his number with some wise counsel to the child beside him."

Grandmother had told me about the lovely lady who had come to look at the house where she had lived as a child. After she had wandered through the rooms and grounds, she had admitted that she had come because she might want to buy it. I don't know whether this was Mrs. Clay-Clopton or another person who had grown up in the house, but I remember Grandmother's reply. She said simply that it had been her home ever since her *own* childhood and that she would never dream of giving it up.

Linka Loveman had actually come to live in that house when she was sixteen. When the state capitol was moved to Montgomery from Tuscaloosa, the fine old capitol building with its classic rotunda had become a famous female academy and Linka had come from her home in Dalton, Georgia, to live with her Aunt Adele and Uncle Bernard to attend that school. Photos from that time show her to be a very pretty girl with wide gray eyes and a big bow on her long fair braids. Even when I knew her, she was still proud of her long wavy hair, which was golden at the ends. I often spent nights with Grandmother when Uncle Hugo was away, and I have a vivid recollection of her in a quaint, high-necked nightgown with long puffed sleeves. When she brushed her hair in front of the tall dressing-table mirror flanked by Meissen cupids, it took almost half an hour.

As a schoolgirl, Linka kept an autograph book filled with saccharine phrases: "May bright angels walk beside you," read one, and an adoring swain of the year 1879, obviously not much of a speller, writes "You are young, you are pretty. You are single, what a pity." A less fervent comment, written one summer during a visit to Chattanooga, said merely, "Another one of your well-wishers." The writer was Adolph Ochs, who later became the founder of the *New York Times*. He was a family friend who had emigrated from Hungary on the same boat with Linka's father, David, and her Uncle Bernard. Young Linka, however, did not choose her husband from any of those young admirers.

During her second year in the house, her adored Aunt Adele, who was her mother's sister and had been brought from Hungary to marry Uncle Bernard, died of pneumonia, which was probably complicated by tuberculosis. As she lay dying, it is said that she made her grieving husband promise that after a suitable time of mourning had elapsed, he would consider marrying Linka, who loved their three little ones and would make them a good mother. And so he did, a year later.

It is hard to say how much of Linka's feeling for Bernard was love and how much was duty. Gentlewomen of her time were brought up with a strong sense of family obligation. However, I do recall Grandmother's telling me more than once, with a great deal of pleasure, that when Grandfather proposed to her he'd said, "Let's link our lives together, Linka, and I will never let you regret it." And she always added to me, "And I never have!"

She had no children of her own, but I believe that her deep feeling for Adele's little ones was the center of her entire life. Especially strong was her love for Hugo, who was only a baby when his mother died. She made Bernard a good and dutiful wife, and her spotless home and delicious meals were a legend. It is a wry commentary on her feeling for her husband that from youthful habit she called him "uncle" until the day he died.

When he was asked why he'd never married, Uncle Hugo used to joke that he could never find a housekeeper as good as his stepmother and I suspect there was more than a grain of truth in that. Up until my grandmother's final illness, a kind of anemia that caused a gradual waning of strength, my father often shared her noon meal because he found in that quiet house refuge from the noisy business world, light years away in atmosphere although only two blocks from the center of town.

The oldest of her foster children was my Aunt Emma, who was only six years Grandmother's junior so Linka was more like a sister than a mother to her. They exchanged many letters filled with recipes and crochet patterns and Emma frequently brought her children from her home in Gadsden for long visits. Emma was a talented artist who drew some fine portraits of both Linka and Grandfather and of the mother she barely remembered.

A visit to Linka was also a refuge for her four brothers and younger sister, Annie, who died tragically very soon after her marriage. One or another of them always seemed to be coming to visit, and I believe she lent them money when they were in need. Her favorite, however, was her poet brother, Robert Loveman, who spent many years of his life in her house. It is said that Linka's rose garden was the inspiration for his best-known poem, "The Rain Song," which begins, "It isn't raining rain to me, / It's raining daffodils." The small volume in which that poem appeared was dedicated to Linka.

Linka nursed Bob faithfully during the long months when he was confined to a wheelchair, and after his death she invested a large sum of money in a privately printed collection of his poems as a memorial to him. During that same year, Grandmother took me with her on the train back to Dalton. I felt it was one of her proudest moments when she attended the rededication of her girlhood home, "The Robin's Nest" as The Robert Loveman Library.

Grandmother's last years were quiet. She had always been a retiring person, but now she saw only her family and her closest friends. My wedding was the last large public event held in her house. To fulfill a childhood dream, I was married at an improvised altar on the wide steps of the formal dining room. The house never looked more beautiful, but during the flurry of wedding preparations, someone suggested that the center table with the marble statue in the parlor be moved into a corner. At first Grandmother wouldn't hear of it, "Why, that Venus has stood right there for forty years!" she objected. It was not until someone suggested that the statue would be in danger of destruction from the crush of guests that she was finally persuaded to move it.

It was moved only one other time—for her coffin three years later. Before her death, though, she got to know her namesake, my first baby daughter, Anne Linka, and she sewed a beautiful silk dress trimmed with tatting for the baby's first birthday. At Linka's funeral, the front parlors were overflowing with flowers, and I had a strange feeling that even the house was grieving for her.

I never went there again without, as Whittier said of his younger sister's death, a sense of "a loss in all familiar things,/ In flower that blooms, and bird that sings."

As I look back on the time I spent in my grandmother's house, I often wonder why her quiet, shy ways held such a great attraction for me. Two more different personalities than ours would be hard to imagine. I was an awkward, tomboyish girl, impulsive, moody and undisciplined, while Grandmother was orderly, serene and practical. Each day's routine for her was carefully planned, varying little from the day before and the day that came after.

My own home was filled with the noisy activity of a large family. Perhaps it was the feeling of permanence in her home that gave my restless nature a needed sense of security. Something of this came to me when I read Melville's lines in *Moby Dick*: "There is deep within each of us an island Tahiti, a green land of peace and beauty in the midst of the cruel sea." Grandmother's house was my green island of peace and beauty.

Chapter Three

Uncle Bob and the Rain Song

Mother's love of books stemmed partly from her determination to keep abreast of world affairs. She sat in on courses in the modern novel and drama and she plunged eagerly into the monthly offerings of her two book clubs. Though she dutifully read every new book, Mother was not really fond of the history selections, nor did she care much for poetry. I later found uncut pages in her copy of Stephen Benet's *John Brown's Body*.

My own deep love of poetry I owe to Grandmother's brother Robert, whom Mother barely knew and would probably not have cared for. Mother belonged to the busy, changing present while Uncle Bob was a shy, gentle figure from the era of the Victorian poets. Grandmother Linka and I had once visited Uncle Bob in his boyhood home in Dalton, but more often I remember him at Grandmother's house, where he spent his last years. With his courtly manners and graceful eloquence, he seemed an integral part of the slightly faded grandeur of the old mansion.

Even as a small child I could sense that the men of the family considered Bob a failure. I think in their eyes he was unsuccessful because he never made any money. And it was a fact that he never really did anything except ramble around in Grandmother's rose garden or in the woods, or talk to people on the street. But Grandmother adored him and so did we children. He had a gay smile and he talked poetry to us in a musical, singsong way as though it were all around us. He made us see things we'd never have noticed otherwise. Sometimes he would take a group of us on a "nature walk" and for the child who saw the most interesting item—maybe a robin's egg or wild strawberries, he would fish a quarter out of his baggy trousers.

I never saw Uncle Bob really dressed up. He wore a loose-flowing tie and shapeless jacket and his thin hair straggled behind his bald pate. Sometimes, too, there was a sweetish odor about him, mixed with his pipe tobacco. Later I recognized it as whiskey, but when I was a child that didn't matter. It was a smell that belonged to Uncle Bob so it was a good smell.

Grandmother was completely captivated by Bob's sentimental and whimsical verse. Although she hadn't the slightest literary facility herself, she was sure he was destined for greatness. She overlooked his weaknesses—his secret drinking and his cavalier scorn of money—and hotly defended him against the more practical members of the family who sometimes rebelled at having to support him.

Uncle Bob died when I was twelve. Nobody knew exactly why—some kind of anemia, they said. He was at Hot Springs when it happened, and I never saw him in his wheel chair. I always believed he had lost an interest in living when he could no longer ramble through the garden and the woods.

Many years later, when I was working for my Master's degree, I selected Uncle Bob as the subject of my thesis. By then, I knew the requirements of scholarship and did a thorough job. I talked to older people who had known Bob as a boy—he was only fifty-nine when he died, so there were still a few of them living. And in Georgia and Alabama I read all his scrapbooks and hundreds of dusty letters. The hundred and four pages I wrote, I titled "Robert Loveman: Belated Romanticist."

Nevertheless, I felt faintly disloyal to that gentle figure—as though I had dissected a wood thrush and pinned it on a board for all to see. I had told his story, the short life with its gay and sad years, but the clear, definitive notes of the song were missing. The Uncle Bob I had known did not come alive in those pages. Yet when I reread them recently, I found that I understood him better. It was true, as I had judged, that he was not a great poet—not even always a very good one—but, in his quiet way, Uncle Bob had struggled all his life for the right to be himself in a postwar age that generally judged a man by the money he made.

I enjoyed interviewing those old-timers who remembered Uncle Bob as a schoolboy and was amused to discover that he had often got into mischief and had received his full share of lickings. He first attended school in a two-room building, with the girls in one room and the boys in the other. Dr. Bitting, who taught the boys, was a fine old gentleman, but had no scruples against using the whip. Moreover, he had a son Paul, whom the other pupils heartily disliked. When Robert Loveman had the misfortune to break Paul Bitting's front tooth with a rock one day, he received a severe lashing but was said to have endured his punishment in true Eton fashion.

Not long after that, an even greater humiliation fell to Robert's lot. It was the custom of Dr. Bitting to make his pupils "speak a piece" every day. Now the doctor had a peculiar aversion to Mrs. Heman's "Casabianca," better known by its familiar first line, "The boy stood on the burning deck." Knowing this, his mischievous pupils plotted to vex him by one and all repeating the detested poem the next day. When the recitation time arrived, Dr. Bitting was regarded with ill-suppressed giggles as the first pupil rose and soulfully chanted the familiar words. Dr. Bitting glared but said not a word. Then one after the other, each boy more nervous than the last, repeated the hated poem. When the tenth boy had finished, the enraged teacher could stand it no longer.

"The next boy who recites that poem," he roared, "will get the worst licking I ever gave!"

The next boy was Robert Loveman! What could he do? On one side was Dr. Bitting; on the other, the anxious faces of his friends whom he had sworn not to fail. Trembling, he arose and once again the heroic words rang out.

Bob was only thirteen when his real struggle for independence began. It was in that year that his Hungarian-immigrant father, who owned a store in the little hill town, took Robert out of school to learn the business. After all, he was the oldest son, and there were six brothers and sisters. Making a bookkeeper out of dreamy, pleasure-loving Bob Loveman must have been a discouraging task. One thinks of Thoreau being forced to make pencils! Bob scribbled poetry on the business ledgers, read dime novels from Ben Gudger's corner "News Depot" or slipped away to the nearby store of a slightly older friend, Will Harben, who shared Bob's literary tastes. Great was old David Loveman's dismay whenever he noticed Bob's absence. "Poet! Vere's de poet!" he would shout, running out on the sidewalk—poet being the most contemptuous term he could apply to his runaway son. Finally his father decided, as Robert had known all along, that his oldest son would never be a merchant. Robert Loveman had won his first battle, and his brother, Sam, became the merchant of the family.

There followed a carefree year of reading law at the University of Alabama in Tuscaloosa where he lived with Linka, his favorite sister. Although the amount of law assimilated in that pleasant year could not have been very great, at the end of the school term Bob felt he was ready to practice. On a visit to Birmingham the following fall, he astounded his brother Morris, who was an established lawyer, by the calm suggestion that his firm be called Loveman and Loveman!

Bob's confidence was not in the least dampened by Morris's lack of enthusiasm. He went on with his plans, although a few casual questions about the nature of the state bar examination were Morris's only clue to his brother's intentions. Opportunity soon came Bob's way in the person of jovial old Colonel Tolliver, a veteran lawyer, who had dropped by to pay Morris a visit and was, of course, introduced to Robert.

The colonel was a very worthy gentleman, but he was inordinately fond of drinking and at that particular time he was a little jolly. Since Bob himself was never one to refuse a good toddy, the liquor was brought out and passed around and in no time Bob and the colonel were talking like boon companions. When the colonel finally left late that night, he was glad to go out of his way to help such a fine, promising young man as Bob Loveman.

In a few days, the necessary arrangements having been made, Bob went to the courthouse to stand for the bar examination. At that time, it was customary for the judge to appoint a committee of lawyers to question each candidate and as Colonel Tolliver had introduced Robert Loveman, the colonel was appointed chairman of the committee which was to question him. The committee withdrew into an adjoining room, where the colonel motioned Loveman to a chair with a smile of recognition. "I'm pretty busy today," he said genially, mopping his wet forehead, for it was a hot September day, and the court room was miserably stuffy.

"Have you read any law, Loveman?"

Loveman knew his man. "No," he replied with an answering smile, "but I know a good many other things." That hit the colonel in exactly the right spot. He leaned back in his chair and roared. "You're competent to practice!" he exclaimed. And thus Robert Loveman became a full-fledged lawyer.

The only vestige that now remains of Robert's short-lived legal experience, however, is a professional card, dashingly adorned with the women's profiles he loved to draw. In fact, one is tempted to suspect Robert of using his bar certificate as an excuse to secure an office of his own in which to compose his poetry.

Before many months had passed, Bob was back in Linka's rose garden, passing the time in his old, happy-go-lucky way. He became a bookkeeper for a few years, this time for his brother-in-law, but seems to have spent most of his time writing poetry or conducting correspondences with women whom he had never seen. These whimsical, charming letters were apparently the nearest he ever came to having love affairs. It may be that Bob felt he would never be able to support a wife, although he loved women, and they, in turn, were invariably charmed by him. Or perhaps in this, as in other areas of his life, Bob preferred the dream to the reality.

Bob's two closest attachments seem to have been to his mother and to Will Harben of Dalton, a tall, spare man ten years older than he. I remember Bob's mother as a plump, serene little woman who was always busy with a piece of crocheting or tatting. She was scrupulously tidy and, like Linka, was renowned for her cooking. She gave the imaginative boy the appreciation and understanding he needed and, for the rest of his life, he was tormented by homesickness and nostalgia whenever he was away from her.

By the time Robert's first little volume, *Poems*, was published by an obliging Tuscaloosa printer in 1893, Will Harben had lived in New York for six years and had already achieved some success as a novelist. In his letters, he kept insisting that Robert join him in the city. However, for two more years Bob remained in Dalton and Tuscaloosa, publishing poems in the leading magazines, seeming hesitant to break away from his beloved haunts. Only when Will Harben married Marybelle Chandler of South Carolina, to whom Robert had introduced him, did he change his mind.

In the quaint New York of the nineties, Robert aligned himself with the more conservative writers—E. C. Stedman, William Dean Howells, Clinton Scollard, Ella Wheeler Wilcox and John Burroughs—rather than with the more vigorous group of young writers making names for themselves like Stephen Crane, Hamlin Garland, Theodore Dreiser, Ellen Glasgow and Edith Wharton. In his leisurely, small-town life, Bob's eyes had remained closed to the turbulent new trends in writing, the "vulgar impertinence" of modern realism. To the end of his life, he would continue to sing his simple songs of the South he loved, unchanged by the New York intelligentsia among whom he now was moving.

Edmund Clarence Stedman helped Bob to market his verse, which was becoming increasingly popular, and Harben introduced him to Mark Twain, Howells and Burroughs, who was to become a lifelong correspondent. When Ella Wheeler Wilcox invited Bob to a reception, he met many other celebrities with whom he attended the theater or art galleries and sometimes exchanged books.

Even a six-month tour of Europe with the Harbens did not change Robert Loveman, although he enjoyed himself immensely. Actually, his European trip was a sentimental pilgrimage to the shrines of all the departed literary geniuses on the continent. Aside from a few mediocre poems, a little serious reading in the British Museum, and a few hours a day studying French, which Bob considered a "melodious language and very easy to learn," the jaunt was chiefly a glorious holiday, financed as usual by his longsuffering family.

At the same time that I chuckled over Uncle Bob's entertaining, carefree letters from Europe, I began to understand why the men in the family complained about the impracticality of their poet. As for Uncle Bob, he had summed up his life—long philosophy in his first little volume in a poem which begins:

> He is a dreamer, let him pass,
> He reads the writing in the grass;
> His seeing soul in rapture goes
> Beyond the beauty of the rose.

Uncle Bob's tragedy lay in the inescapable fact that, devoted as he was to poetry, he never really created much that was fresh and new. All his life he had steeped himself in the romantic poetry of the past and unconsciously imitated the thoughts, form, and even the mannerisms of the writers he admired. Only for a few short years, when he persuaded his mother, then a widow, and his younger sister, Annie, to come and live with him in New York, did he create any enduring work. Now the cheerful, comfortable atmosphere which always surrounded his mother and the stimulating influences of his New York literary contacts were available to him simultaneously.

In later years, when he toured the South with his Robert Loveman Concert Company—consisting of himself as poetry reader, a harpist and a girl singer—Bob was fond of recounting for audiences the manner in which he came to write the song that had made him famous. His room, overlooking Central Park, was in the attic of the building. On the night that he wrote the "Rain Song," he lay awake for a long time, listening to rain drops on the roof. While he was trying to go to sleep, the musical lines of this song kept running through his mind. Then the words came to him. Afraid to trust his memory, he got up, lit a lamp and wrote the "Rain Song."

> "It isn't raining rain to me,
> It's raining daffodils;
> In every dimpled drop I see
> Wild flowers on the hills.

> The clouds of gray engulf the day,
> And overwhelm the town;
> It isn't raining rain to me,
> It's raining roses down.
> It isn't raining rain to me,
> But fields of clover bloom,
> Where every buccaneering bee
> May find a bed and room.
> A health unto the happy!
> A fig for him who frets!
> It isn't raining rain to me,
> It's raining violets."

The popularity of the "Rain Song" spread like wildfire and the words of the song were on all lips soon after it appeared in the April 1901 issue of *Harper's Magazine*. Uncle Bob had at last obtained some of the recognition he had always dreamed of! It hardly seems believable nowadays, when poets seem to write primarily for other poets, that such an unpretentious little song could have captivated people's hearts so much, but those were more sentimental years. Even H. L. Mencken, the king of acerbic critics, whom Robert had met in Baltimore the previous year, wrote to him, "I envy you the day you wrote the 'Rain Song' and every other man with music in him must envy you, too." Though Mencken and Loveman seldom saw each other, an enduring friendship grew up between them, as both scorned the trite conventions of society and both were confirmed lovers of good music, German, and "good fellows."

When I was six years old, I memorized the "Rain Song" to please Uncle Bob and I always loved it, as did most children. It was, in fact, included in children's grade school literature books for many years and is still a favorite. In 1970 it was also featured in the Third Book of a new linguistics program of the Roberts English Series published by Harcourt, Brace and World. Several lines of the poem were plagiarized in the well-known popular song, "April Showers" made famous by the late Al Jolson. When enraged friends finally persuaded Uncle Bob, indifferent as always to money, to write the publishers, he never received a reply or a penny of compensation from the enormous sale of that hit song.

As I grew older, however, my own favorites among Uncle Bob's poems were those in *The Gates of Silence*, published in 1903. It was this collection that caused men like Mencken and William Dean Howells to see in Bob a gleam of real promise. Mencken wrote him, on receiving an autographed copy:

"Some day—I have been planning it for a long time—I hope to do an article on these beautiful songs of yours. But you know how difficult that is; to convey the charm of poetry is impossible in prose, and so one is reduced to the manufacture of mortar between quotations."

The poems in *The Gates of Silence* have a pruned simplicity of tone and wording which makes them far superior to his earlier work. They are, above all, poems of questioning, of doubt, and of an indefinable fear of the unknown.

> One by one the gods we know
> Weary of our trust,
> One by one the prophets go
> Dreaming to the dust.
> All the cobweb creeds of men
> Vanish into air,
> Leaving nothing save a 'When?'
> Nothing save a 'Where?'"

The optimistic idealism of Bob's youth transformed itself into a wonder that sometimes approached pessimism, making him ask:

> "Why think the soul survive its clay
> Even an instant's span?
> What beacon holds aloft a ray,
> Presumptuous, proud man?"

And there is one poem that seems a foretaste of our own fears in an atom-haunted era:

> All else of Man is dead, and I
> Stand lone upon the sphere;
> The pale earth shivers, sigh on sign,
> And shakes with frenzied fear.
> Some Titan tears the world apart,
> And sets the seas to rout,
> And I, a silence at my heart,
> See the cold sun fade out.

My own favorite is a more hopeful poem, born of Bob's deep love of Nature. It was the favorite also of his friend John Burroughs, the great naturalist, who requested that it be read at his funeral. It begins:

> I could not see till I was dead;
> Then, through the mold and wet,
> A rose breathed softly overhead,
> I heard a violet.

I am sure Uncle Bob was thinking of Grandmother's rose garden when he wrote those lines, and when I walk there today, I feel very close to him. His last years were sad ones, although we children were not aware of it. I hope our heedless games and thoughtless teasing brought him some small comfort in his grief. For, during the short space of two years, he lost his lifetime friend, Will Harben, his adored mother, and his lovely young sister Annie, who had kept house for him in New York until her marriage. Saddest of all, perhaps, Bob lost his ability to write poetry. His later poems, all three volumes of them, were stilted and old-fashioned, all the spontaneity and gaiety gone. Scarcely more than a year after his mother's death, Uncle Bob became ill and never recovered. One of the most revealing of his later poems begins:

> My heart was burned out long ago,
> My bosom is a waste of snow,
> And lonely as a pale lagoon
> In the dead mountains of the moon.

Yet, when I remember my Uncle Bob in these later days, as I often do, it is not with sadness. Nor do I think of him as a failure, although his poems are almost forgotten. When my own daughters were small, I once bought them an illustrated gift book—*Rhymes for Children*, I think it was called. With a thrill of recognition, I found in it a big picture of a little girl with her nose flattened against the window pane as the rain poured down. And my children's voices echoed mine in the familiar words,

"It isn't raining rain to me, / It's raining daffodils."

And they had thought him a failure! My heart was full of love and pride when I recalled the shabby little poet with the beautiful smile and musical voice who had taught children to see beauty where they would never have seen it otherwise.

Chapter Four

Steamboat Whistle

Although in some ways Mother neglected us, she at least granted us the independence which she sought for herself, although I don't suppose she intended us to run away on a steamboat. We climbed trees, played Cowboys and Indians with our friends, or roamed the woods and along the river bank. Guild's Woods, which we often visited, was a place of mystery and excitement. The woods began across the railroad at the foot of the hill and ended—most wonderfully—at the river.

We were, of course, forbidden to go near the river, a command which made it irresistible. Dark tales of drownings and whirlpools during the spring floods only whetted our appetites. The one house on this riverbank domain belonged to the dour lock-keeper and was perched on high pilings, in case the water rose. In front of the house stood the great lock gates themselves and we could see and hear the monstrous roaring of the water over the dam.

The magic signal that always set us in motion was the deep-throated moan of the steamboat whistle summoning the lock-keeper to open the gates.

"Listen, Sam!" I screamed to my eight-year-old brother one day. "There goes the boat whistle!"

Sam appeared at the foot of the cellar steps, brown mud on his arms up to his elbows as he was in the process of digging a robber's cave into the dirt wall of the cellar.

"I jus' can't go now," Sam informed us. "It's mos' big enough to get inside of already."

"Well, go on and dig your ole caves, then! We'll go see the boat, won't we, Mary?" I took Mary's hand and pulled her toward the back fence but she looked dubiously at the woods.

"Mama was real mad las' time I played down in the woods with y'all. She said I couldn' play over here any more if I went again—'cause there's *tramps* on the railroad track!" She spoke the last words in a hushed voice. Mary did not know exactly what tramps were, I am sure, but they must be terrible if her mama was frightened of them.

I could never think of anything convincing to say when Mary introduced her mama into the argument, so I stood silent, knowing that the steamboat would slip down the river in a few minutes, and then it would be too late. I wondered why grownups never could seem to understand it was much nicer to play in the woods and along the river bank than in a pokey little backyard.

Suddenly Sam, who had been listening to the argument, had a change of heart and ran up the cellar steps. "I tell you what, Mary! The tramps jus' come on the *railroad* track and the place where we're going is way on the other side!" He had forgotten the robber's cave, lured by the steamboat whistle.

I could see that Mary was almost convinced when at that moment the boat whistle sounded again, starting in a long moan that was low and thick at first, then louder and deeper, and finally wailing off into a hollow echo. For one tense moment the three of us looked at each other while it died away, then like a flash we were off down the hill.

Mary had to stop on the railroad track to pour the sand out

of her sandals; then we were in the cool woods, darting across smooth, slippery pine needles and catching tantalizing glimpses of the river through the trees. The woods ended abruptly on the edge of a green meadow that sloped down to the river bank. When we stopped there to catch our breath for the final run, Mary shaded her eyes with her hand.

"I see it! I see it!" she squealed in her excitement. It hadn't even started into the lock yet so we could see the shiny orange smokestack a little to one side of the lock-keeper's gray cabin.

"Hurry up so we can watch them let the water down," Sam called, racing off. It was the greatest puzzle to him how the water inside the lock gates could rise slowly up or down. I was more interested in the foaming wheel behind the steamer. It always frightened me a little.

Sam had already crossed the swinging bridge when we reached the bottom of the slope. This was a little narrow bridge swung on wire cables across the gulley. Mary was terrified when she saw it, but I laughed.

"See? It won't hurt you," I called to her as I ran out to the middle of the bridge and began jumping up and down so the bridge started swinging violently. Mary began to cry.

"I'm goin' home," she moaned. "I don't like shaky bridges."

Sam came back across it. "Aw, don't be a baby, Mary! Look, I'll carry you across!" Mary took one look at Sam's stringbean legs, then at her own round ones and began to laugh, but she didn't move.

"Now, you just watch me, and we'll go across so it won't shake a bit," Sam told her.

Finally Mary swallowed hard, clutched the rails with both hands, and followed his lead by putting down one and sliding the other up to it.

"See?" Sam said proudly. "It didn't even jiggle!"

The bridge was soon forgotten and we stood awestruck at the

full view of the steamboat waiting outside the lock gates. We crept closer and closer down the steep bank, the boat a magnet drawing us to it. Silently we watched a ragged Negro cross and recross the gangplank that rested on the bank and disappear inside the engine room. Soon they'd pull it in and the big skeleton wheel would start to turn. Then the lock gates would slowly open.

Barrels and crates littered the boat's deck but in the stern a piece of canvas had been thrown across two barrels, creating a little shelter. "Wouldn't that be a nice playhouse?" I asked Sam, pointing to it.

I could see the mischievous look in his eyes, but nobody dared to speak first. Not a soul was in sight on the little steamer and the men on the lock were busy working the iron handles that would open the gates. "We could slip on—real quick—an' then get off soon's it gets inside the lock gates. Reckon they'd catch us?" Sam asked.

For answer, I ran over the gangplank, grinned from the deck at the other two, and hid under the canvas. After casting one look at the dirty driftwood lapping the side of the boat under the gangplank, Mary, to our amazement, tiptoed gingerly across the shaky boards, but Sam had barely settled himself between the barrels when the ragged, barefooted Negro crossed the stern, in plain view of us, to inspect the wheel. We held our breath. Apparently satisfied, he went back along the deck. Safe in our canvas retreat, we watched as the blades of the big wheel began to churn the muddy water into white froth. The wooden deck was vibrating so it made our teeth chatter as the boat chugged slowly into the lock, then shuddered to a stop. Then as we watched, fascinated, two men in greasy coveralls closed the gates behind the boat by pushing the big iron handles round and round. Never before had we seen this process from such close range. We could even count the iron shelves on the inside of the gate as the water slowly began to sink, leaving one shelf after another wet and dripping.

Suddenly Sam turned and faced Mary and me. "Say, it's 'bout time we got offa here!" he said, but we could barely hear him because of the rumble of the water pouring over the dam.

I peered out at the lock's cement walls towering above us, so close that we could touch them. "There's a ladder," I whispered.

Sam looked at the slimy water under the ladder, then glanced doubtfully at Mary who was just beginning to comprehend the full danger of our position.

"Let's get off quick!" she gasped. "I don't like boats."

"Ssh," I warned her as she'd raised her voice.

We had just started to creep out from our hiding place when the sound of heavy footsteps coming along the deck toward us sent us scurrying back. We heard a hoarse voice bellow out, "Hey, Jim! Go fix that pipe!"

Terror-stricken, we cowered under the canvas. Mary had begun to cry, but Sam silenced her with a scornful look. Then an enormous man in a dirty blue shirt came into our range of vision and spit tobacco over the railing. He stood scowling at the dark water as it slowly sank to the level of the river below the dam, and we began to have awful visions of his wrath if he should find us. The steamer had begun vibrating again and I could see the foam from the wheel glisten in the sun. Still the man stood there, a black scowl on his face.

When the boat was clear of the lock, the man finally stalked off down the deck. We looked in terror at the ever-widening expanse of water between the lock gates and the revolving wheel. I lost all my courage and composure. "I'm scared," I whispered. "I wish we hadn't come!"

"And who started all this I'd like to know?" my brother snapped, not looking as brave as he would have liked. "Anyway, we can't get off now . . ."

The little quarrel relieved the tension in the air and the motion of the boat was soothing. The sun beating down on our canvas roof made us feel drowsy. After all, we decided, it was rather fun being on a boat and not knowing where we were going. Sam's spirits began to revive. "What if we go all the way to—to Mobile," he suggested slyly, grinning at the look of dismay on Mary's face.

"Oh, we wouldn't have to," I said knowingly. "There's another lock 'bout a mile down river." Mary was relieved.

"It's like being on the ocean," Mary said with a sigh, and we nodded agreement although the river was as vast as anything we could imagine. Looking back, we saw the lock had already disappeared around a curve.

The novelty of the adventure wore off, however, as our canvas shelter got close and hot. My foot had gone to sleep, and I longed to stand up and stamp it. Sam and Mary were fussing about who was taking up the most room and unconsciously raised their voices. We didn't hear the steps of the fat captain as he sauntered toward us. It was a sulky, perspiring trio that met his amazed eyes when he pulled off the canvas!

For a long moment the captain gazed at us—Sam's arms spotted with mud and axle grease, my dress streaked with tar, Mary's cheeks grimy with tears. Then the captain laughed, throwing back his head and roaring until the tears came into his eyes. Sam gave a sickly grin, but Mary and I were almost as frightened by his guffaws as we had been by the scowls of the deckhand.

"What's this?" wheezed another voice, and a shrunken old man shuffled into view. He, too, cackled when he saw us.

"Wal, if that ain' too much!" And he slapped his leg. "What'll we do with 'em, Cap'n? Throw 'em overboard?" He winked broadly at the captain.

"We've got to get rid of 'em, sure enuff," said the captain more soberly. "Hey, you Jim up there," he called to the wheelhouse.

"Shove her in to shore!" Then he turned to Sam. "What's the big idea, young fella—runnin' off with these girls?" The captain and the old man still seemed to think this was a good joke, but Mary began to cry, and Sam looked sheepish. Twisting my fingers, I mumbled, "We'd like to get off, please, Sir."

The boat was already turning toward shore and they shoved the gangplank on land when we were close enough. The captain waved and shouted goodbye to us as we stood forlornly on the river bank and was still chuckling as the boat steamed slowly into the river again. Without a word, we trudged mechanically up the slope toward the railroad track. Then, as we climbed to the top of the last hill, we saw the wide, aproned figure of Mammy and heard her wailing plaintively, "You chillun bettah git yo'sevs on up heah befo' I tell yo' mama you done run off ergin."

Mammy could always be cajoled with a few hugs and promises. She didn't want to admit she was getting too old and crippled to keep track of us.

Although the stolen steamboat ride was our most memorable adventure, there were many other times when Guild's Woods was the center of our games. We would dare each other to go through the slimy culvert under the railroad track, where our make-believe swords poked hesitantly at the myriad spider webs around the openings. I braved that nightmare journey once, but still shudder at the sight of a spider. We frightened ourselves, too, with tales of what we said was quicksand. There was a bed of stinking, sucking mud in one of the ravines near the river which we poked sticks into and sometimes pretended to be caught in the mud, but whether it really was quicksand we never found out, although I did lose a shoe there once and had to limp home.

The most chill-producing secret of Guild's Woods, though, was the skeleton cave. We made up so many stories about the cave that we came to believe them, at least partly. Actually it was not a real cave at all, but an overhanging rock ledge too narrow for one to stand under and too deep for one to see to the back of the recess. A very brave child, crawling halfway inside and peering into the dimness, could barely discern the outlines of the "skeleton." For all I know, it may actually have been the bones of some poor animal. More likely it was an old stick wedged there by a long-ago flood. Anyway, we never found out. The mystery was more fun than dull reality.

As we grew older and the neighborhood boys and girls formed tight little circles, the woods became the scene of trailing games and treasure hunts. Many a clue was written in blood, the edges of the paper carefully burned with stolen matches. Then there were the sled races. Having no snow for winter sports, the boys went sledding down the sides of the ravines on the thick brown carpet of pine needles. They were slippery enough, but the ride became dangerously fast when the homemade wooden sleds were well-greased with lard. At the bottom of the run, the sledsman was unceremoniously dumped into a strawstack and would emerge sneezing furiously.

I shared in all those games, but the woods didn't really belong to me except when I was alone. Childhood is not always a happy time, I think, although it may seem that way when measured by adult grief. The times when I grieved over broken friendships or felt unwanted and unloved, I went to my special place where the other children never played. The path led through tangled blackberry bushes to a sluggish stream overhung by branches. Safe in my favored tree, I'd let the silence seep into me until the outside world was far away. Then I'd become aware of the secret life of the woods—an orange-streaked moccasin sunning on a limb, a specklebreasted thrush, the transparent wings of a dragon fly. Even years afterward, the memory of those woods is soothing and lovely.

Chapter Five

Mammy Was Not a Myth

Mammy came to us when I was about to be born. In those days, babies in our town were delivered in their mothers' bedrooms, and lucky was the young matron who could secure Mammy as a midwife, because she was the best of them all and had helped deliver the offspring of many of our prominent families. However, Mother grew so attached to Mammy that she could not be persuaded to let her go, so Mammy stayed on and on through the years, a loved and honored member of our household.

About twenty years later, when my youngest sister, Peggy, was in her teens and the Depression had caused great financial loss to my father, Mother told us one day, "Well, I guess we'll just have to let Mammy go. She's too old to work and I can't keep a cook because she bosses them around so. We'll let her visit her son in Texas and maybe she'll want to stay . . ."

Such an uproar ensued that Mother hastily abondoned the project, but eventually a compromise was reached. Mammy was well fixed financially. She had occupied our best upstairs bedroom for years, and, with all her physical and medical needs supplied by my parents, she had invested her salary in two rental houses which yielded her a steady income. Discerning our predicament, perhaps from our long faces, Mammy herself suggested that she stay on without salary. She "allowed as she wasn't much account no more no way" and that all she needed was "backy" for her corncob pipe and Sundays free for visiting.

On Sundays "Aunt Caroline," as the colored community called her, removed her enormous apron and put on her good black dress. With a long, black-headed pin she fastened a hat over her gray hair and she pulled black gloves over the swollen, rheumatic joints of her yellow hands. At last, proudly ensconced in the family car, she was driven to the neat home of her granddaughter Stella, or perhaps to the house of her pastor, or that of the well-to-do undertaker. Her colored friends felt honored by these visits and she was much in demand, for everyone loved and revered her.

At the time of the crisis, Mammy was perhaps in her eighties. I say "perhaps" because she herself didn't know when she was born. "I just turned into my teens at the time of the 'Mancipation'" was all Mammy knew "for certain sure." With a child's curiosity about those faraway days of slavery, I had asked eager questions, but her answers were always scanty and her recollections dimmed by the years.

She had been born, Mammy told me, on the Taylor plantation on the far side of the river, but she didn't remember her mother, who had been sold down the river when Mammy was a little girl. Years later, when I was presumed old enough to understand, Mammy whispered the name of her white father who was the overseer of the plantation. Mammy was proud of the fact that she was a "house slave," not one of them no 'count fiel' han's." Mammy had shared a room with her small mistress who had become her inseparable companion.

I used to beg over and over for the story of how Mammy had avoided a "lickin'" by hiding under the voluminous hoop-skirts of her "Big Mistress," whose sense of decorum forbade the lifting of the skirts to apply the peach switch. Often Mammy described the "goodies" in the boxes that the Master brought upriver from Mobile at Christmastime, the store-bought shoes and the surprise packages for each child. I think my favorite story, though, concerned the time Mammy was almost kidnapped.

Mammy had got into some mischief—she "disremembered" what but thought it was swiping cookies—and she had decided to hide out in the corn crib to avoid being punished. When it was almost dark and she judged enough time had passed for Big Mistress to have forgotten her sin, Mammy slipped out of her hiding place. To her dismay, at the very moment she was climbing the split-rail fence, she looked up to see "a big red Injun sittin' on his horse." Some Indians had been camped near the plantation awaiting removal to the reservations in the West and he was one of them. Some of the farming Indians owned many slaves and were reputed to be hard taskmasters. The direst warning Mammy could recall from her childhood was, "You better look out, or the Injuns'll get you!" Now the terrified child thought the day of judgment was at hand. With one hand, the big Indian grabbed Mammy off the fence and threw her across his saddle. However, he hadn't counted on such a battle. The little girl kicked and scratched and screamed until finally she slipped free and escaped. For my benefit, Mammy always added the moral to her story, "An' that was the las' time I was ever a bad girl!"

Mammy became the self-appointed moral preceptor of my younger brother and me. Our parents were not churchgoers, and deeply disturbed over our being brought up "like little heathens," Mammy set herself to make amends. Sometimes she took us to her own church, where we sat in the front row among the friendly colored people, listening with delight to the fervent "Amen, Brothers" and the singing. More often, however, before her rheumatic knees began to fail her, Mammy sternly marched us across town to our own Baptist church while our remiss parents were still having their Sunday sleep. Mammy's faith was deep-rooted. She talked to God all day, usually out loud, and we had no doubt that He answered her.

"Dear Lawd," Mammy would say, turning her eyes upward, "you see dis chile, how she actin'. Make her behave herself, Lawd!" To support the pleas to the ever-present Lord, she would sometimes remove her false teeth—which she often carried in her pocket anyway as they did not fit well—and shake them at us. I am sorry to say that, as far as we children were concerned, those disembodied teeth were more effective than her appeals to the unseen Maker. When we became a little older and braver, however, we would make a game of it and tease her.

"Shake your teeth at us, Mammy," we would beg, "please, just once!" If she complied, we would run screaming from the room in pretended terror. Then we would laugh uproariously, Mammy loudest of all. Laughter was always close to the surface with Mammy, and though her aching knees induced long, pleading conversations with God or "blessed Jesus," she usually ended her complaints with a chuckle at herself.

"Blessed Jesus," Mammy would beg, "he'p me climb dese steps! Why you give me dese no 'count knees'" At the top of the offending stairs and seated finally in the armless rocking chair where in babyhood she had comforted us all, Mammy would, likely as not, burst into quavering but joyous song, in tune to the creaking of the rockers. "Will there be any stars, any stars in my crown . . . In that glo-o-rious home up ab-o-ve!" Mammy's heaven was a certain thing; it had crystal gates and golden streets, and the blessed little cherubs were all the babies who had died.

One summer afternoon when I was old enough to drive Mammy on her Sunday visits, we drove out the unpaved, winding river road to search for the location of the plantation where she had lived as a girl. Mammy's pale eyes, filmed over with cataracts, peered from behind the dime-store gold-rimmed spectacles she always wore. Eagerly she scanned the barren fields for a familiar house or tree, but we found none. She seemed to remember a partly toppled, unpainted church we passed and she thought the old house would have been "a little piece beyond." I stopped the car at the spot she indicated, and we got out, standing on the dusty roadside. Erosion had done its work well. A vast gulley stretched as far as the eye could see, its upper edges still crumbling from the recent rain. There was nothing to say. We climbed back into the car and I turned it toward home.

It was either that day or a little later that Mammy told me what had become of her first little mistress. She had gone insane. I have often longed to know the details of the story, what happened in those sad days of poverty and Reconstruction, to the young girl Mammy remembered as being always gentle and kind and whom she had loved enough to follow into the asylum. That was how Mammy had become a nurse. Unable to let her little mistress go behind the barred windows alone, Mammy had gone to the doctors, begging them to let her stay, too, and to teach her how she could help.

The doctors had trained her along with the white nurses, Mammy told me proudly, and she had found she had a "knack" for the work. The doctors always called on her to attend the difficult or violent patients, because Mammy could "jolly them out of it," as she expressed it. She hated the straitjackets and restraints, she said, and had *never* needed to use them on her patients. She told me many stories of the hospital, some of them hilariously funny. However, she never spoke of her little mistress' illness, and I never asked. I only know that several years later Mammy left the asylum and became the private nurse to the head doctor's own wife, starting his four children on their journey into life as later she started the four of us.

Another subject I never asked about was Mammy's husband, or whether she had one. I remember the mild shock I experienced when I overheard the tag end of a grownup conversation that suddenly ceased as I entered the room—"and even with our own Mammy, we don't know that there ever *was* a 'Mr. Baker.'" The question hung unanswered in the room.

I know that Mammy had had six children, and that they all had contracted smallpox. George, the oldest boy, had been delivering groceries to some people who had the disease. He himself escaped the dreaded ailment, but I suppose he blamed himself for bringing it home to his family, because he ran away "up Nawth" and wasn't heard from for years. During the illness of her children, Mammy blessed the good doctors from the asylum who each week brought baskets of food to her gate and instructions for the children's care. Despite her faithful nursing, however, Mammy's only daughter and two of her boys died. Only the son in Texas, the runaway George, and her baby, Ernest, survived.

I never saw Ernest, but I knew him well through his letters, which it became my duty to read and to answer, as Mammy, to her great sorrow, could neither read nor write. These rambling, misspelled, but affectionate missives arrived each week from the tuberculosis sanitorium in Chicago where Ernest was a patient. Like George, he had "gone Nawth," but his journey had ended in tragedy. His letters, however, were always optimistic and reflected a faith as trusting as that of Mammy. Everyone was good to him, he said, and he was sure God would let him get well by Spring; he would walk into the house and surprise her one of these days. The letters grew shorter and farther apart until the day the telegram came and Mother read it to her,

On that day—I must have been about seven then—I came home from school to find Mammy clutching the upstairs railing with one hand and the dreaded yellow paper with the other. Tears were running unchecked down her cheeks as she rocked to and fro in her agony, calling out over and over, "Dear Lawd, blessed Jesus, why you take my baby? He never done nothin' bad—all his life—not *nothin*!" It was my first lesson in sorrow. In all my childhood mishaps, Mammy had been my serene and unchanging source of strength. Now she was stricken, and I stood there unable to help her.

It was during the period of her mourning that I conceived the idea of teaching Mammy to read. "If I could jus' read dose blessed promises for mysef," she would say, "dat I can see my boy up yonder."

One day I brought my primer and a magnifying glass into her room, and our lessons commenced. I was already an omniverous reader because my mother, a former first-grade teacher, had taught me when I was three. By the ripe age of seven, I had rambled happily from Grimm's and Hawthorne's fairy tales, through *Gulliver's Travels* and *Robinson Crusoe* and had started school in the third grade. Now I was determined that my Mammy must learn to read.

The details of that long struggle are now hazy in my memory, but I do remember the turning point—the gift from her friend "Miss Mary" Moody, whose babies Mammy had helped deliver, of a beautiful leather Bible with large print. I shall never forget Mammy's radiant face when she first read aloud for herself the promises of *Revelation*: "And the twelve gates were twelve pearls and the streets of the city were pure gold." She had the most wonderful expression of all when she read, "And God shall wipe away all tears from their eyes; and there shall be no more death, neither sorrow nor crying, neither shall there be any more pain ..." God had not forgotten her after all. He had sent her a personal message. Thereafter she no longer needed my services as teacher. The reading of the Good Book became Mammy's nightly ritual and her unfailing comfort.

A happy time came during my teen years when the prodigal son George returned from New York, a happy time for Mammy because she had almost given him up for dead, and a happy time for us because he became our cook, and an excellent one at that. As my mother often complained, it was almost impossible for us to keep a cook who could meet Mammy's scrupulous standards of cleanliness and courtesy. Now, providentially George, who at some time during a colorful career had been a short-order cook, returned. Soon, loud but good-natured arguments were coming out of our kitchen as Mammy initiated her tall, intelligent-looking son into the mysteries of flaky pie crust and the delectable small hot biscuits we all loved.

We never inquired too closely about George's missing years—he hinted once at a brief smuggling episode on a rum-runner—but I managed to elicit some stories of his days as a vaudeville entertainer. Persuaded to demonstrate his talents, George did a wonderful limber-jointed "buck-and-wing." Sometimes he seated himself in a chair placed on top of the kitchen table, balanced the chair on one of its legs, opened a newspaper lengthwise and balanced it diagonally on the tip of his nose. The first time I saw that I was captivated. After that, George entertained many teenage gatherings at our house. By that time, George had moved into the renovated "servant's house" in our backyard. Having a venturesome, restless nature, he was soon bored with the humdrum household routine, but he dearly loved parties, when he would put on his spotless white coat and do the honors to perfection.

George's skill as a yardman also transformed our small back garden into a New Orleans-style courtyard complete with fish pool, flagstones and high rock wall. Adjoining that wall at the back of the garden, however, was a tall hedge which George had to keep trimmed. The regular trimming of that hedge led to an incident which piqued my mother but greatly amused the rest of us.

One day George was taking longer than usual to trim the offending hedge. I heard my mother's angry voice in the garden below and leaned out an upstairs window to see what was happening. Then I laughed out loud. To relieve the monotony of his task, George had neatly clipped our family name in letters a foot wide and half as high in the *top* of the hedge where, as my father chuckled with delight, they could only have been seen from an airplane!

George's artistic temperament often strained my mother's disposition. Nevertheless, Mother later had cause to appreciate another facet of his nature when her elderly father suffered a stroke which made him a semi-invalid. Having no downstairs bedroom where Grandpa could be cared for in our house, Mother loaned her sister in Birmingham the services of George as valet and nurse. It soon became evident that George had inherited Mammy's "knack" with the sick and helpless, and George became indispensable to Grandpa, remaining there for years.

When Grandpa died, we thought George would come back to us, but by that time he had become a leader among the Negro people of Birmingham and had, in fact, been elected president of the Negro Elks Club. He also had a remunerative job as bartender in Birmingham's oldest country club, where his convivial nature made him a general favorite. I saw him only once again after he left us. About ten years ago when my father died, George came by train from Birmingham for his last visit to our house. Gray-haired and dignified in his good black suit, George accompanied the family to the funeral, and it gave us all great comfort to have him there.

When I had gone away to school in Atlanta, I'd return on vacations to find Mammy still her cheerful self but each time seeming a little more feeble and shrunken. Then a sort of miracle occurred. I don't pretend to understand it; I can only tell what happened.

The summer after my freshman year at college, Mammy spoke of a knot in her breast. Fearing the worst, we hurried her to our doctor who soon confirmed our fears that the growth was cancerous. We did not tell Mammy; she wouldn't have understood. The doctor operated but the malignancy had spread too far. It had penetrated all her vital organs, he told us, and she would have only a few months to live.

We decided to continue as though nothing were amiss, although we did all we could to make Mammy happy. Miraculously, Mammy's health began to improve and when I returned home from my sophomore year, she seemed stronger. "Sometimes these cancers arrest themselves," our doctor explained. "We don't know why." Six years later Mammy was still there to smile at my wedding, although her once sturdy figure had grown very wispy and frail. In the end, the steep stairs proved her worst enemy, and finally she could no longer conquer them. Sadly, we agreed with her granddaughter Stella that Mammy should move to her front parlor.

This was a large, pleasant room on a quiet street, near enough to the sidewalk for Mammy to chat with passers-by. We visited her often, partly to assure ourselves of her comfort, but chiefly because we missed her. After her twenty-seven years in our house, her departure left a great emptiness.

When my first daughter was born in Montgomery, where I had moved after my marriage, I could hardly wait to show her to Mammy and her delight in the baby was all I had anticipated. On this visit, however, I was saddened to find that Mammy stayed most of the time in her great carved walnut bed, although she was still able to care for her bodily needs and to prepare her simple meals on an electric plate. She said over and over again that she was in no pain—"jes don' have strenth in dese ole laigs!" I was not to worry about her, Mammy said, her hand caressing the baby's yellow curls. "Jes' think, Miss Helen, heaben'll be full of precious little cherubim and seraphim jes' like dis one! All dem sweet little babies like I used to nurse! I cain't hardly wait to git up dere."

The time was not far away. On my next visit some months later, I was told that Mammy had contracted pneumonia and had been in a coma for two days. I hurried to the house but at the door Stella shook her head sadly. "She won't know you, I'm afraid. She hasn't recognized anyone for days. Listen to her." A harsh, whistling sound seemed to fill the house, the sound of Mammy's breathing. Her thin face was devoid of any expression, her eyes were closed. Yet I felt I had to try.

"Mammy," I told her, "I've come to see you." There was to be one more miracle, born of love. Mammy opened her eyes and held out her arms, with smiling lips and a catch in her voice.

"Bless you, Miss Helen, I knew you'd come! I knew you'd come!" She died in my arms.

Chapter Six

Our Homemade Automobile

Our homemade automobile was not the first car we owned. Daddy had been fascinated by automobiles since his college days when he and his brother Hugo had been the proud owners of one of the first in town. The account of their trip on a sixty mile jaunt to Birmingham in that vehicle had even been written up on the front page of the newspaper.

Daddy thought automobiles had a great future, and, as head of the city commission, he had succeeded in pushing through a bill to pave the main street despite the violent objections of old man Fitts who knew for certain that the paving would damage the hoofs of the carriage horses. Daddy had even patented his invention for what he claimed to be the improvement of motoring—a set of canvas and celluloid car curtains guaranteed to snap into place in minutes. When not in use, these curtains were stored in handy pockets attached to the canvas top of the car.

My brother Sam and I had many occasions to test Daddy's invention on our semi-annual shopping trips to Birmingham. It was the custom of many Tuscaloosans to purchase such important items as shoes and winter coats from the large choice of merchandise in the big city department stores. There was a hushed air of excitement and anticipation surrounding the preparations for these journeys, since we would be awakened long before daylight, and creeping downstairs in the cold chill of early morning darkness had something of the atmosphere of Christmas. Then, abruptly, the stillness would be shattered by cranking the automobile—a feat accompanied by a shuddering series of bangs and gurgles. Actually, starting the car must have been a rather dangerous undertaking. I recall hearing talk of Uncle Hugo's Willie breaking his arm doing it, and I remember Daddy once refused to fire an unsatisfactory yardman because "he was so good at cranking up." Finally though, everything was ready, the picnic lunches packed, the extra gasoline and tool box stored in the trunk—literally a small trunk attached behind the spare tire—and Daddy's gloves, cap and coveralls placed under the back seat—and we bounced and chugged off into the dawn.

We soon became very familiar with that dusty old one-track road to Birmingham. There were few places in it wide enough to pull to the side if we had to stop for one reason or another. The first puncture usually happened right after we had left civilization completely. Mother would wait impatiently with her "I knew it" expression, but Sam and I were interested spectators as Daddy swathed himself in coveralls, cap and goggles and removed various instruments from the toolbox to jack up the car. After he had prised the tire loose from the wheel and had patched the leak with an evil-smelling substance, there would come the more difficult chore of getting the tire back on the wheel and pumping it up again. Sometimes we helped by standing on the obstinate tire, and occasionally we would be allowed to put the lug screws back on. Mainly, I suspect, we were a nuisance, as we invariably wandered to explore the countryside, and our parents had to round us up before we could continue the journey.

After the first three or four punctures, the novelty wore off, and by that time, we were frankly bored and began to devise various games to pass the hours. One game was "stamping" road-widening signs, "R.W.'s," we called them. These were lettered cement markers placed at intervals to comfort travelers with the hope that some day the narrow track would be two-laned. I would yell, "That's one for me!" and "stamp" the marker on my side of the road by licking my right thumb and banging the heel of my right hand into the palm of my left. Sam did the same on his side of the road, and then we would quarrel over who had seen the most road-markers. When we were tired of that, we would "stamp" mules or cemeteries, almost anything of which there was a great number. Where the road was narrow, Sam and I would lean dangerously out of the sides of the open car to try to catch a leaf or twig.

At this, Daddy would bark at us to stop it and Mother would wail, "Oh, if just once I could take a trip without children! I don't believe we'll ever get there!"

If a shower started, as it invariably did, Sam and I were told to make ourselves useful by putting up Daddy's snap-on curtains. At first this task was fun, but there were drawbacks which soon exhausted our enthusiasm. In a hard rain the curtains usually leaked at the seams and when the sun came out again we would always have a debate about whether to unhook them or to leave them up. As it was a messy job to put on the coveralls and fold up the now damp curtains, Daddy would usually settle this argument by saying there'd probably be another shower pretty soon, so we'd better leave them up. I can still smell the mingled odors of baked celluloid, dust, seat leather, and sweat as the noon sun converted our back seat into an oven. We were usually a subdued and sulky crew when we finally arrived in Birmingham.

Our destination was always the Tutwiler Hotel, whose large ground floor restrooms were our oasis. I was intrigued by putting a nickel in the slot to open the toilet door, but cross because Mother wouldn't permit me to insert another nickel in the machine that miraculously sprayed out sickeningly sweet Jade perfume.

During the ordeal of shopping the only things we liked were the elevators. The high point of the trip as far as my brother and I were concerned was the choice of desserts from the array of meringue-topped wonders at the Britling cafeteria. "Sam, they'll be sick if they eat all that stuff! Why do you let them get it?" Mother would protest. However, trips were Daddy's province, and on a tour he was expansive and indulgent. We were always two overstuffed children slumbering among the clothing boxes through the punctures on the homeward journey.

Sometime later, Daddy bought a self-starting car. I think it was about the same time that we purchased the electric victrola, which also dispensed with the cranking-up process, and in front of which we spent hours lying on the floor listening to Fritz Kreisler's violin, John McCormack's golden tenor, the dulcet Italian of the "Quartet from Rigoletto" and the "Sextette from Lucia." My favorite records, though, were Paul Whiteman's "Song of India" and the Hawaiian ukelele tunes, to which my spend-the-day friends and I loved to improvise dances with my mother's Spanish shawls and discarded finery.

Radio must have started about that time, but it had little effect on our lives then as those early crystal sets were likely to squawk and screech. The most exciting acquisition, however, was our first closed car. Those cars had been in production for some time, but they were very expensive. After much thought, Daddy conceived the bright idea of having the garage man weld the top of a wrecked closed car onto the body of our open touring car. The resulting vehicle's appearance was rather top heavy and the throaty-sounding horn that went "O - oo - ga!" still remained on the outside. Yet the car looked wonderful to us as it meant the final demise of the frustrating snap-on car curtains. Now we could travel in style!

It was not unusual in those days for family cars to survive many seasons of constant use. My bachelor Uncle Hugo lovingly polished his eight-year-old Cadillac every day, gloating over comments that it looked "like it was brand new." And the longevity of Daddy's homemade, closed car was phenomenal. It refused to die. Years after we discarded it for a modish new model, it was still rattling through the streets as a Negro taxicab. To its already strange-looking exterior the new proprietor had added a coon tail, a rabbit's foot, and various other appendages. On many an occasion when I was with my high-school friends, the beat-up old relic would heave into sight, preceded by its plaintive "O - oo - ga!" Somebody was sure to recognize it and yell, "Hey, there's your car! Let's hail it for a ride!" I endured agonies of embarrassment as my companions roared with laughter.

No doubt there are some who long for the good old days of travel. Not I! Give me the timesaving speed of a jet or the comfortable smoothness of a modern, airconditioned car. It may be true that we have lost some measure of such intangible human qualities as dignity, charm and grace in the sometimes hectic pace of modern life, but the revolution in travel and communications has changed the face of the globe, and I'm glad that I have lived to share in that evolution—from those ancient autos to the astronauts.

Chapter Seven

GRANDMOTHER LONGSHORE

As I have said, Mother did not really like children, and I suspect the vacation trips she most enjoyed were the ones she took after we children were away on our annual visit with Grandmother Longshore in Columbiana. Mother's real problem was getting us there, for Daddy flatly refused to share this ordeal, and who could blame him! The train trip that was such an exciting adventure to us was the bane of Mother's existence. For a journey of less than a hundred miles, we had to change trains three times. First there was an hour-long wait in the sooty Birmingham station to board the smaller train for Calera thirty miles further along the line.

Here we waited again for the once-a-day local to Shelby Springs, the now almost abandoned "watering resort" of mother's youth. Countless times on each train, our long-suffering mother would have to wipe cinders from our eyes with her once-clean handkerchief. When we got bored sitting on the stiff red plush seats, we manufactured errands to the restrooms or the ice-water tank just to scrutinize our fellow passengers.

By the time we reached the last change of trains, the one Mother most detested and the one we most enjoyed, she would be flushed and dishevelled, almost in a state of collapse. During this last five-mile lap of our odyssey, we rode on homemade wooden benches that occupied half the single boxcar which was the only transportation linking the sleepy village with the outside world. I will not say we deliberately harassed Mother, but her disapproval of our behavior somehow encouraged us.

Our arrival in Columbiana was especially exciting because a good portion of the town's population would be waiting at the station in wagons, carriages, or on foot. This gathering was not in our honor, of course—everyone went there for the high point of the day, when the mail was called out from the open door of the other half of the boxcar. But this was only one of many fascinating events for us town-bred children.

With my youngest aunt, Louise, who was my age, we hunted for smooth, warm eggs in the vast, cobwebby hayloft, or tried to cling to the slippery backs of frisky calves. Also we spent many hours constructing a mud dam across the shallow branch at the bottom of the pasture in the vain hope of creating a swimming hole. Despite all our efforts, the muddy water barely reached our knees, for Columbiana, alas, had no river, not even a creek! The well water tasted of lime, too, to which it took some time to get accustomed.

For matters like washing the girls' long hair, there was a big rain barrel by the kitchen door, but one of our greatest treats on a hot summer day was the free-stone water from the deep well on great-grandmother Longshore's back porch. To get there we had a long walk down the tree-shaded road, carrying our empty buckets and scuffing bare feet through the soft, hot dust. Sometimes we would be lucky enough to hitch a ride on the tongue of a mule-drawn wagon to the unpainted clapboard cottage on the low hill, its picket fence around the bottom and Aunt Lou's poodle guarding the swinging gate.

Great-grandma was nearly a hundred and sometimes didn't seem to notice us, but on her good days we were permitted to tiptoe to her big, high bed in the front room and look at her stereoptican slides. Then gentle Great-Aunt Fanny, who was very deaf, and Great-Aunt Lou, who was tall and thin with a long, mournful face and black hair, would take us back to the kitchen for thin sugar cookies and dippers full of sparkling, sweet-tasting water drawn up from the shadowy depths of the famous well on the back porch. Once refreshed, we were ready to start home with our full buckets. We never considered those errands as chores because it was taken for granted at Grandmother Longshore's home that all the children had jobs to do.

Mine was to clean the chimneys of the kerosene lamps my aunts and uncles brought with them downstairs each morning to the table in the ell. The summer I was seven I was given that delicate task, but it was hard for small hands to push the soft cloth inside the fragile glass tops and slide it back and forth to remove the smoky film. Louise preferred to help Grandma get breakfast in the kitchen across the hallway, but I liked to stand at my post in the cool, open-ended passage and feel the big, rambling house come slowly to life as the family brought down their night pails and dirty linens and made their morning visits to the outdoor privy. I also knew that if I did my task well, Grandma would let me help churn the butter and pat it into the wooden molds, which was my favorite task of all.

By the time I came downstairs, Grandma would have been busy for hours. The breakfast coffee had been roasted and ground and the fruits and vegetables had been selected from the garden and the fat slabs of bacon brought from the smokehouse. I could already smell the aroma of the hot biscuits rising in the wood stove's big oven while on top of the ice-chest beside me in the ell would be the cooling bowls of oatmeal. I always felt a little envy because Grandpa got the biggest bowl with a layer of sugar half an inch thick. I didn't envy him his bowl of clabber, though, since that was one country delicacy I never learned to like.

Before Grandpa and the boys were called in to breakfast from their chores in the barn, I had to run quickly to the parlor to choose a blessing in the well-worn family Bible, as it was a Longshore custom for each person to repeat a Bible verse after Grandpa's morning prayer. We did not often say grace in my city home, and I didn't know the Bible phrases that my aunts and uncles did. Usually I picked the shortest verses, "Jesus wept," or "God is love," once in a while venturing a "Suffer little children . . ." or one of the "blesseds."

"Blessed are the meek" was one verse I knew applied to Grandma. Now when I look at a picture of her, I see that she had a thin, plain face under the smooth wings of brown hair, that the joints of her capable fingers were swollen and that her cotton house dress hung shapeless on her slight figure. Yet, when I was a child, her kind expression and calm gray eyes were beautiful to me. A moment before the blessings, she would slip briefly onto the edge of her chair at the foot of the long, white-clothed table, ready at an instant to bustle back to the kitchen for hot platters of eggs or china boats of white flour gravy. She was always serene and quiet with the result that people felt that way themselves when they were near her, no matter how they had felt before.

I suppose that was why this big family never seemed to quarrel—at least not when Grandma was present. In all my summer visits to Grandma's home, I can't remember a voice being raised in anger. When my stout, florid Grandpa talked to God, it was in a firm, confident voice as he demanded God's blessings on the family gathered there to praise Him. Yet when Grandpa urged Grandma to sit down and eat before her food got cold, his voice was softer, and he tenderly called her "Niffan." He had created that pet name for my small, slender Grandma out of her name,

Fanny, turned around because, as he said, she "wasn't any bigger than a niffan."

After breakfast Grandpa, who was probate judge of Shelby County, walked down the shady street to his office in the domed white marble courthouse. The five oldest children were away that summer. Two of my aunts had jobs in the city, and my mother and two others were married. But all six of the other Longshores were home that year. One of the boys, Will, was a judge, too. He didn't walk to work, however, as he was the proud owner of the only car in Columbiana, a resplendent Model-A Ford two-seater with which he toured his circuit of the neighboring towns. Will was a quiet, shy man, and I liked him as much as I liked his car.

The youngest boys, Paul and James Rowe, were quiet, too, although I don't recall their being often in the house. Usually the two played baseball and swam with the other teenage boys in the muddy creeks of nearby towns. I do know that tall, blond Paul was the only one of the boys who would ever help Grandma with the flower garden she was always trying to find the time to cultivate. I gratefully recall how Paul once rescued Louise and me from an angry bull when we'd wandered into the forbidden five-mile pasture. Uncle Leslie, the only dark-haired one of the family, was its gayest member. He was courting the girls that summer, and the rich baritone with which he accompanied his mandolin strumming and the mischievous sparkle in his eyes made him a favorite with them. However, the family spoke of Leslie in worried whispers because he was determined to learn to fly one of those newfangled airplanes when it was time for him to be called up. He did learn, too, a year later, but much to his disgust the Armistice was signed shortly before he was to go overseas.

Frances, the only girl at home besides little Louise, was on the threshold of being a young lady. Fair-haired and freckled, with rather plain features, she bustled with efficiency. Being at an assertive age, she would occasionally protest Grandma's casual organization of her household.

"Mama, why don't you make those lazy boys get up and weed that garden?" she'd demand as Grandma toiled among the rows of vegetables while upstairs her tall sons slept late. But Grandma never *made* anyone do anything. Mild and softspoken always, she inspired others by her own example.

I think Frances actually enjoyed her orgies of housecleaning. The big, fluffy featherbeds would be put out to sun, the white iron bedsteads repainted, and the wooden trundle-beds beneath would be pulled out and rubbed with kerosene. Frances chose those jobs because it suited her nature—as her sister Alice made all her own clothes because she liked to sew. My mother, who disliked sewing, had never been made to learn.

Grandma had a simple and uncomplicated faith that if she did her part, the Lord would provide. I remember one afternoon when, as was her custom after the noon meal, Grandma was resting and reading a magazine in the square front parlor with its ugly Mission furniture. Frances ran into the room breathless but managed to exclaim, "Mama, the garden's just about petered out except for tomatoes. What in the world are we going to have for supper?"

Completely undisturbed, Grandma answered quietly, "The children can go down to the store for cheese, and we'll have a nice Welsh rarebit with sliced tomatoes." She then quoted one of her favorite Bible passages about the lilies of the field.

Louise and I liked to go to the store on the rare occasions when Grandma sent us because we were given pennies to buy hard candies out of the big dusty cases. The sticky red and green balls often tasted slightly moldy and the colors came off on our hands and tongues but it didn't matter. Grandma's whole life revolved around her family, and she rarely had visitors, but in town something interesting was always the center of talk. There was the perennial contest, for instance, between two townsmen with large families of girls as to which wife would first produce a son. Large wagers were laid as each approached the anticipated blessed event, but, every year that I remember, those two women gave birth to girls.

The most exciting event that happened while we were in Columbiana was the time when the hardware store caught fire. Local gossip noted that these fires conveniently broke out whenever the owner's debts were larger than his profits, but no one could ever prove anything. Everybody loyally turned out for the bucket brigade to protect adjacent property, and it made us feel very grown-up to take our places in line and pass the heavy buckets to the waiting men. I also felt very noble because I despised the store owner's sons, an unwashed group of foul-mouthed boys who were always waiting to waylay us and whisper their dirty stories.

Bedtime came early at the Longshores' home and seldom did anything happen in the evenings except the Wednesday night prayer meetings. On one momentous occasion, however, we were allowed to attend a traveling Chautauqua performance in a huge tent on the courthouse lawn. This event attracted many strangers to town, including a traveling evangelist. As there was only a vacant lot between the courthouse and the Longshore front porch, we could clearly hear the singsong of the preacher's voice as he shouted his message from the court house steps, "Come and be saved, EVERYBODY! Come, come, you SINNERS, come to the arms of JESUS . . ." The cadences rising and falling in the summer night mingled with the sounds of katydids and perfume of the climbing honeysuckle.

Before going to bed, it was the custom of the family to gather in the parlor for evening prayers. Someone would light the big Coleman lamp on the center table and pump the flame into white brilliance. Then Grandpa would settle his spectacles and reverently open the big Bible for the nightly reading. In the long prayer afterward, he would mention each absent child and bless him by name. On one memorable occasion, Grandpa intoned a prayer for William Jennings Bryan, who was then engaged in the so-called "Scopes monkey trial." The silver-tongued Bryan was a special hero to my Baptist grandparents, and I am quite sure they pictured the embattled Darwin, who had dared to question Man's divine creation, as an instrument of the Devil himself.

Later, when I learned more about the mysteries of science, I looked back with wry amusement and a certain condescension at the simple creed of my grandparents, wondering how a man as learned in the law as Grandpa was could have held so rigid a view. Grandma, of course, never questioned Grandpa's correctness on that or any other matter. As I retraced their early struggles in a region impoverished by war and reconstruction, an area almost barren of schools, I began to understand.

Grandpa's father and three older brothers had been killed in the Civil War, leaving his mother to support the half-grown boy and his three sisters on her munificent widow's pension of thirty dollars a month. Grandpa had somehow managed to attend two years of college at Washington and Lee, after which he had "read law" in a local office, as was then the custom. Grandpa greatly revered education, however, and he toured Alabama making speeches in support of free public schools and acquiring, incidentally, a considerable reputation as an orator.

Grandma's education must have been scanty indeed, for she had married when she was only fifteen. By that time, she had lost not only her father, killed in an unnamed Texas battle, but also her childhood home, which had been burned down. I have been told that Grandma and Grandpa had vowed on the altar that their children would have the college education they themselves had been denied. Of their twelve children, one died in boyhood, but the remaining eleven all proudly earned their diplomas. I find it almost impossible to imagine the patient labor and stubborn self-denial my grandparents must have endured to achieve that goal.

Grandma's one hour of rest in the afternoon was the only idleness she ever permitted herself. It was a standing joke in the family that by the time the young Negro hired girl arrived in the morning, Grandma would have finished all the heavy work and there wasn't much left for the girl to do except to help with the ironing. One of the small rooms on the kitchen side of the ell was reserved for this purpose, and I vividly recall the mound of snow white clothes, fragrant from sun and starch, that almost reached the ceiling. Even here, Grandma did the most difficult work, for her sons were convinced that nobody except "Mama" could iron their shirt collars and cuffs to the requisite stiff perfection. I often think of Bible verses when my grandma comes to mind because they came so easily and naturally to her lips, but there is one that seems particularly fitting. I never hear the familiar description from 31st Proverbs of the virtuous woman who "riseth while it is yet night" and who "looketh well to the ways of her household" without remembering that mountain of clothes in that hot little room.

As the life of this family was centered in the church, Sunday was a very special day. First we heard the mellow sound of the morning church bells tolling across the meadows. Even the air seemed different—the sun more golden, rustle of silk dresses being shaken out of wardrobes more exciting, the blessings longer at table, and the pervading air of hushed expectancy more intense. One Sunday I shocked Grandma by asking that she sew my dress jacket where I had split the seam in my hurry to be ready for church. "We must never use a needle on the Lord's day," she told me. "Here, I'll pin it for you, and we'll fold it like this and it won't show a bit."

Grandma had a way with children, and they invariably loved her. For forty years, Grandma guided the little ones of the Cradle

Roll department in the small clapboard church down the hill, and it was said that Grandma never missed a Sunday except when she was having her own babies. Grandpa, meanwhile, was superintendent of the Sunday school, where he directed the affairs of the church as he did those of the county—but he never mixed the two. Once an unfortunate young preacher referred to one of the political parties from the pulpit, whereupon he was startled to see my grandfather rise from his front seat in the congregation and inform him, "Young man, in this church we don't mix politics and religion!"

Though he was sometimes stern, Grandpa was jovial and loving with children, and his own little ones often vied for the privilege of sitting on his broad lap. For them, as for Grandma, he had made up his own pet names; the six little girls were "little Voisamoms" and the six boys were "little Tempafells." Yet it was to gentle Grandma that we children turned to dry our tears and solve our problems.

Many times, when in the throes of my own children's problems, I have tried to fathom the secret of Grandma's serenity. At times, too, when I have been questioning and doubting, I have envied her calm acceptance of her burdens. Once it crossed my mind to wonder what she would have thought of the atomic bomb, and I seemed to hear her soft voice saying, "Sufficient to the day is the evil thereof," and to leave such questions "in the lap of the Lord." We lived in different worlds, Grandma and I.

Her own world of Columbiana was changing rapidly even during her lifetime. Honking automobiles stirred up the dust, poor folks were drifting into town from the surrounding hills and, one by one, the old established families had moved away to the cities. The Longshores had always held themselves a little aloof. I had never heard Grandma glorify her family tree, but she let her children know they came from "good people." When later I traced the Longshore family, I found that the Terrells, Chiles, and Clarks of Grandma's ancestry went back in an unbroken line to Quaker records of the late 1600's. I discovered that the first Euclydus Longshore had arrived with William Penn on the good ship *Welcome* and that, in Virginia some years later, Christopher Clark and his sons and the Quakeress Sarah Terrell had freed their slaves for reasons of conscience. They were indeed "good people."

Grandma said in later years that when the younger children came home from school pronouncing "white" and "nice" with a long 'i' like the hill people, she felt it was time for the Longshores, too, to move to the city.

I was a busy college student when my grandparents settled in the industrial town of Gadsden and somehow I never found an opportunity to visit them there. Later, I was heartsick about this, because Grandma died not very long after the move, but I drew some consolation from a talk I had with a Gadsden woman who lived on the same block. She would always remember my grandmother, she said, because of her beautiful flower garden and the lovely bouquets she shared with everyone in the neighborhood. I was grateful that after those busy years, Grandma had finally found time to cultivate her garden.

Chapter Eight

Our Reluctant Suitors

From the very beginning of the twenties, my familiar world had been changing fast. Daddy had made a big land sale, and our rambling old house had sprouted into modern splendor with French doors, stuccoed arches and tiled bathrooms. My old sleeping porch and the nursery had also been remodelled past recognition. It was all very exciting, especially the new seven-passenger Buick with jump seats. Although I was only thirteen, I had been driving the car for a year now, as I was big for my age and there were no drivers' regulations in those days. Mother had developed the habit of sending me on errands she disliked. I accepted those tasks, as I felt very grown-up when I was behind the wheel of the big car.

    I was proud of the new living room, too, but the house seemed to be constantly full of people and noise, as Mother had begun an endless round of cocktail parties which I disliked. My burgeoning curiosity about the adult world to which I had formerly paid little attention and had even scorned was a sign that I was a victim of adolescence. Although in earlier days we had giggled over the booklets about "the birds and the bees" which our anxious mothers had given us to read, my friend Mary and I now examined with minute attention the colored illustrations of the miracle of birth in her doctor father's medical books. We began to be aware of boys, too, and both conceived a secret crush on Hudson Strode, then a handsome young student boarding in the neighborhood. We practised the various fraternity "whistles," using them to signal each other, and shamelessly hid behind Mary's parlor drapes to spy on her older sister when she entertained her date on the porch swing. Finally there arrived the day of the confession.

It was one of those rare times when I had the car for the entire afternoon while Mother played golf at the new country club. With Mary, I started out to collect my friends. Mary and I had been "playing out" in the summer evenings with a new arrival in our neighborhood, a merry girl with black hair "stiff as a horses' tail," as she put it, and a freckled face. We called her Tutter, for sister, as her three brothers did, and her house was our first stop. Then we honked joyously at the houses of Winkie and Sarah Sims, with whom we had been "spend-the-day" friends for years. Now that we had a car, we could travel further afield, and recently had begun to include pretty, blue-eyed Sarah Holmes, whose mother liked young people and was often inveigled into chaperoning our various outings. Last there was Hermione, a small, vivacious chatterbox who always added excitement to our little group. She lived a whole mile away, near the university, and her mother took in students to board.

After we had made the usual circle around the flagpole in the middle of town, we drove past the campus and out toward the insane asylum. There the pavement ended and the dirt road took a small but steep rise over the railroad tracks which we loved to drive over at top speed. Driving over very fast gave us that same sinking feeling in the pits of our stomachs as a roller coaster.

Having navigated "the hospital bump" to the squealing satisfaction of the group, I turned the big blue car through the beautiful hospital woods into a narrow track called Lovers' Lane by students and natives alike. Hermione interrupted our gossip session with an announcement. "Be quiet, everybody!" she screamed. "I want to say something. If I don't tell somebody, I'll . . . I'll just burst!" Startled into momentary silence, we stared at her. Covering her flushed face with her hands, Hermione moaned, "I don't know how to say it. Promise you won't laugh!"

We promised eagerly. "It's just . . ." Hermione began. "It's just . . .I like boys! I mean I'm really *crazy* about boys! It's all I can think about!"

We looked at each other, not knowing what to say, until Sarah offered, "I know just how you feel. I feel that way, too. I guess all of us do, only we didn't dare come right out and say it."

We all nodded, feeling deliciously secretive as though bound in a solemn sisterhood, exclusive and perhaps forbidden. In the babble of confession that followed Hermione's proclamation, we realized that although we confessed to a liking for boys, they were not even aware of our existence, and that somehow that unhappy state of affairs must change.

"We could have a party," Winkie suggested. "Only maybe the boys won't come! Tutter, do you think Jeff could get them to?"

Jeff was Tutter's brother who played ball with some of the West End clan. That select group shared the double glory of being experts on the football field and of being the objects of our parents' shocked disapproval at their ignorance of the social graces and their atrocious grammar. Remote and godlike, those boys were our heroes and became the object of our campaign.

"Mother did promise me a party for my birthday," Tutter said. "I'll ask her if I can have a 'prom,' and I'll start working on Jeff. But you've all got to help. Every one of you has to tell me who to invite to be your partner!"

In the excited plotting that followed I had my first foretaste of fear. That autumn I would be in high school, having skipped two elementary grades, while my friends were still in junior high. Frantically I catalogued my scanty list of male acquaintances. Then, not wanting to be a spoilsport, I pushed the problem to the back of my mind.

The girls had begun on a favorite subject—Mabel. With her yellow hair and pouty lips, she was the envy of our group because she already had a beau. In fact, the white clapboard farmhouse, which Mabel affected to hate, was a favorite rendezvous for all the boys old enough to drive. "She just crooks her little finger and all the boys come running!" Sarah Sims wailed.

"Well, Mabel's not fast, if that's what you're thinking!" Tutter interrupted hotly. "She's my cousin, and I know her better than anybody. She's just pretty and knows how to get the boys to talk to her. You're just jealous, all of you."

I wasn't sure what being "fast" meant and decided it probably had something to do with kissing. I began to wonder what I would do if a boy tried to kiss me. A chuckle from Tutter focused my wandering attention. "Did you hear what Pal wrote Mabel the other day?" Tutter asked. "He's working on his uncle's cattle farm down in the black belt this summer and you know how Pal is about animals?"

We nodded. Pal's menagerie was notorious, the latest addition being a large, defanged rattlesnake. "Well, his uncle gave him a heifer to raise," Tutter continued, "and he named her Mabel! Pal thought it was a big compliment, but Mabel was furious. She said, 'If he thinks I look like a cow, I'm not ever going to speak to him again.' She'll have to make up with him, though, because I'm putting Pal's name on her prom invitation."

After the laughter that followed, we settled down to the absorbing task of choosing our own partners. When the dreaded moment arrived, and Tutter asked whose name to put on my card, I had my answer ready. "Anybody who's left over will suit me," I said airily.

"I'm not choosy." I was relieved to put my worrisome problem in the hands of the others because in the competition for beaux I had an insurmountable handicap. I had bumps!

Sometimes my face would be smooth and clear and on those rare days, I would strike smiling poses in front of my bedroom mirror and dream of someone who would find me beautiful—someone, perhaps, like Malcolm or Keith, the two little knights in my favorite Little Colonel books. Then, on a day when I longed to look my best, the hated bumps would reappear, as if they had a malignant desire to spoil my fun. I am sure it disappointed my mother to have a shy and awkward daughter with bumps instead of a dainty little feminine creature with golden curls and a string of beaux. Mother sent me to her beauty parlor operator for facials and mud packs, and when that did no good, I was forced to endure a series of X-ray treatments. Nothing worked. When the day of my first prom arrived, I looked in the mirror, steeling myself against despair. There were the bumps, punctual as always! Wiping away the angry tears, I flung on my party dress without a backward glance at the cruel reflection.

Tutter's front porch and parlor seemed crowded only with girls. I couldn't see any boys at all. Then they surprised us, laughing and joshing, all clustering around Mabel. She was pretending to be furious at Pal about the heifer, but from the way she looked at him, it was obvious she was only teasing. I found a place beside Tutter's mother, a large, pleasant woman with Tutter's brown eyes and a comfortable manner. She told us that Jeff would be there in a few minutes with some of the West End boys and then they'd start the promenades.

The girls exchanged excited glances and whispers, and presently the slamming of car doors and loud voices announced the new arrivals. The boys crowded together in the doorway, looking tall and muscular behind Jeff's short, sturdy figure. The party came suddenly to life. There was noisy laughter and much shoving as the boys located their partners. When someone distributed the promcards to the girls, I clutched mine in a perspiring hand, afraid to turn it over. Maybe the girls hadn't found a partner for me after all.

At the moment I finally summoned courage and found the name, Jim Snow, he materialized beside me. He was a tall, studious boy in my own grade, and I watched gratefully as he scrawled his name on the first and last spaces of my card. Then he courteously steered me around the room until, miraculously, there were only two blank spaces remaining on my card when the bell rang for the first prom. Tutter's mother called cheerfully, "You'll have ten minutes—just time to walk to the corner and back. No sitting in cars, and be on the porch when I ring the bell!"

Jim firmly grabbed my elbow and took off with such giant strides that I ran beside him, gasping for breath and trying desperately to think of something bright to say. Unfortunately—or fortunately, for me—Jim had a habit of stuttering. He'd barely managed to stammer out a sentence or two before we were back at the porch, and he was saying, "Th - th - thank you for the w - w - walk, and here's your next p - p - partner."

Flushed and confused, I managed to survive the remaining proms. I had a few terrifying moments toward the end when an older boy who had the reputation of being a girl-chaser pushed me into the front seat of Jeff's Model-T Ford that was parked at the curb and promptly draped his arm around me. As I pulled away, protesting, one of the West End boys yelled from the sidewalk, "I see you there, Charles! Since when did you take up cradle-snatching?"

Grateful for the interruption, I escaped, but my relief at arriving safely on the lighted porch turned to dismay as I looked at my prom card. The next two places were blank! For twenty minutes

I would be on my own.

My first idea was to go upstairs to hide in Tutter's bedroom, but as I approached the stairs, I saw the eager faces of her small brother and sister peering through the bannisters. Not wanting to run that gamut, I went toward the back hall and lingered in the shadows near the kitchen door, longing for a magic cloak to make me invisible like the man in the fairy story. Then suddenly, through my fog of despair, I heard my name mentioned. Tutter's mother and father were sitting at the lighted kitchen table sipping coffee and chatting about the party. "But Helen is my favorite," Tutter's father was saying. "She's going to be a good-looking woman some day!"

On such small things do we build our worlds. How many times I hugged to my heart the words of that gentle, graying man! His comment sustained me during the recurrent ordeals of my high school years: the hated and persistent bumps, the "break" dances that followed the proms and during which I invariably managed to get "stuck" whenever I was tapped by a desirable partner, and most difficult of all, the fact that although I had a few admirers, I didn't have a real sweetheart.

Youth is resilient, however, and I found compensations for my shyness and the awkward times. My house with its spacious living rooms and the electric victrola gradually became the gathering place for the crowd on Friday nights, and two of the sought-after West End boys became regular members. They went everywhere together— Diddle, tall and thin with big ears and a deep voice, and Bo Mack, short, good-natured and full of noisy fun. Sometimes we grew too boisterous, as on one occasion when some of the boys were pulling each other on the scatter rugs over the waxed floors, Mammy would appear at the top of the stairs in her nightcap and roar down at us, "You chillun better cut out dat racket, er I'm goin' tell yo' mother how you messin' up her house!"

At first Mammy's appearance had a dampening effect, but Bo Mack soon discovered, as my brother and I had found long ago, that Mammy could be wheedled into good humor. Bo Mack would climb the stairs and drape his arm around her stooped shoulders, "Now, Mammy, we're just havin' a little fun, and we'll clean up real good. Be a good sport, huh?" Mammy would soon be chuckling in spite of herself.

Bo Mack was hard to resist, and more than one of the girls determined to capture his attention. Soon I became a sort of big sister or confidante to each one in the crowd, relaying messages or patching up quarrels. As we were too young for single-dating, our fun, noisy as it was, was harmless. Mostly we sang. All of us had ukeleles, and Bo Mack and Diddle loved to harmonize. When we rode around in the boys' rattletrap cars, the quiet streets would echo to the tunes of "Shine On, Harvest Moon," or "I wish you were jealous of me, Dear," or the boys' special favorite, "Oh, gypsy lady, won't you be my baby?"

I had only one rigid rule for parties at my house, and it was well known and respected—there was to be no drinking! Only once was the rule broken and then not by one of our crowd but by an outsider, a university boy. It was in those days an unwritten but no less effective dictum that a girl who showed the slightest interest in the college students would soon find herself extremely unpopular with the high school boys. During my last year in high school, however, an attractive, dark-haired college boy named Frenchy became smitten with Mabel. The more she refused to date him, the more determined he was to break down her resistance.

One night when my parents were away, I invited six of the girls for a spend-the-night party. We amused ourselves by teasing Mabel about her new conquest until we realized that she was actually quite upset and almost frightened of him. "What am I going to do?" she moaned. "I've told him I won't see him, but he telephones me every night. I just know he'll call tonight, and they'll tell him where I am. Gosh! What if he comes over here?"

"Surely he wouldn't come without being asked?" I ventured.

"He's likely to do most anything," Mabel wailed. "You just don't know him! And the bad part of it is, I can't help but like the fool!"

"Listen, Mabel," Winkie suggested practically, "if does come over, we'll protect you. Just slip upstairs, and we'll tell him you aren't here."

Mabel proved a good prophet. No sooner had we settled down to eat a late snack from the well-stocked refrigerator than a knock sounded at the front door. "I'll go," Mary volunteered, "and if it's him I'll talk long enough for you to slip upstairs." Winkie, Sarah, and I huddled behind the pantry door to wait for Mary while Mabel and Tutter rushed for the stairs. Mary returned. "It was him all right, but I don't think he believed me. He kept saying, 'I know she's here. They told me she was here!' And I'm sure he's been drinking!"

We gasped and looked at each other, then tiptoed cautiously to the door and peered outside. The street was dark and empty. Mary shivered. "I don't know why, but I've got a feeling we haven't heard the last of him. Let's go upstairs with Mabel and Tutter."

While we undressed for bed, we joked about our fears for Mabel's sake, but I think none of us was surprised a little later to hear the crash of glass and a mellow but slurred voice calling, "Mabel, I know you're up there. Pleash come down jush for a minute!"

"Oh, Lord!" Winkie wailed. "He's in the house! *Now* what?"

Then Mabel surprised us. "I'll go down and get rid of the idiot. He can't do any harm with all of you here, and it's a cinch he can't stay in the house!" Before we had recovered our wits, she had flung a coat around herself and started down the stairs. We leaned over the bannisters listening to the murmur of voices until

Mabel finally reappeared.

"I feel awful about this, Helen," she said. "I don't know what you can tell your parents. He broke a pane out of the French door to get inside and cut his hand pretty bad. He was bleeding all over everything so I tied up his cut with his handkerchief. He's promised to behave himself, so we can just hope he'll go on home now."

We complimented Mabel on her neat disposal of Frenchy and settled into drowsy conversation in the pulled-together beds. However, the redoubtable Frenchy had not yet exhausted all his ammunition. As I was about to drift into sleep, I heard a melodious yodel from the garden below our window, "Girl of my dreams, I love you - ou - ou, Honest I do - o - o, You - ou - ou are so swe-eet!"

"Oh, no!" Mabel cried, running to the window. "Go home, Frenchy!" she called down. "We're trying to sleep!"

"I'm jsuh sheranadin' you, Mabel," Frenchy answered sweetly. "Nothin' wrong ith that!" He continued the serenade despite our pleas.

Help came from an unexpected source. Across the street lived Dr. Barnwell, the formidable dean of the English department. A short time later we heard a police car arrive and looked outside to behold the dean's tall, white-haired figure at the curb, clutching his bathrobe with one hand and pointing an accusing finger toward Frenchy, who was frantically trying to dispose of the evidence. Wise in the ways of the bathtub gin generation, he knew that if he were arrested "in possession," he'd have a much harder time. Alas for Frenchy! For his desired encounter with Mabel, he had fortified himself with a gallon jug of "white lightning" and nothing would make the liquor pour out quicker. He was caught red-handed—literally, since it was still covered with blood—and carted off to jail with his half-filled jug!

Fortunately such eventful nights were rare, although, like all teenagers, we sometimes got into mischief. We saved up our allowances to buy copies of a vulgar joke magazine called "Captain Billy's Whizz Bang" which gave us a secret thrill of naughtiness, we went together to see Clara Bow in "Flaming Youth," we learned the Big Apple and the Charleston, we horrified our long-suffering parents by going in a group to the men's barber shop to have our hair "pineappled" into boyish bobs, and we experimented with cigarettes, although we never dared smoke them openly.

For this latter pursuit, we formed a short-lived association called the "Down Club," the object of which was to drive outside town to smoke. The first member who spotted an approaching car would yell "Down!" at which signal we would all hastily duck into the smoke-filled interior of the car, to emerge choking and coughing when the danger had passed. Luckily we tired of this pastime, and most of us didn't take up smoking until we were much older.

We formed a more enduring club, one full of happy associations, soon after my friends joined me in high school. Ostensibly the club met to play bridge, and, as this game was popular with our parents, we had their blessings on our efforts. Actually, however, the bridge games usually degenerated into gossip sessions, with eight eager girls vying for the floor until someone would scream, "Listen, y'all, please let's bid! I've got my first good hand!" Then the chatter would quiet briefly, to break out again moments later.

It was at a meeting at Sarah's house that we conceived the idea of having a dance—a real one at the country club—with engraved invitations and a big-name orchestra, a dance that would be the crowning event of the year and a memory forever. For such an affair we needed a name for our club. After a long argument, Sarah's mother supplied the winning appellation. We delighted in calling Sarah's mother by her maiden name, Mary Darling. "Why not the Comus Club," she suggested, "like the famous Mardi Gras club in New Orleans? You know Comus was the god of fun and laughter and that's what your club is for!"

Immediately, the newly christened club was deeply involved with preparations for the great event. It was my last year in high school, but the approaching graduation assumed a distant and shadowy place in my mind when compared with the Comus Club ball. Club meetings became a battleground between Sarah and Hermione, each bursting with ideas for which she was eager to win support. We all agreed on one thing; we were determined to have a popular Birmingham orchestra. Though shocked by the—to us—enormous price of a hundred and twenty-five dollars, we plunged into money-making projects in which rivalries were soon forgotten. Out of the chaos and confusion, gradually our dance took shape.

It was a perfect evening, even for me, since for once the detested bumps failed to appear and we had invited many more boys than girls so there were partners to spare. Hermione had planned a revolving spotlight that decorated the long ballroom with changing patterns of soft colors as we danced to the melting strains of swing music. We had ruled out the jerky Charleston steps as being out of place on that dignified evening. The saxophone began the plaintive notes of "Girl of My Dreams" for the Comus Club "no-break" leadout, and when my chosen partner actually complimented me on my dancing, my happiness was complete.

I floated through graduation and its attendant functions in a reminiscent haze. After our triumphant dance, everything else seemed dull and anticlimactic. I couldn't bring myself to contemplate the future which seemed impossibly fuzzy and far away. Then one day, with no warning, the future was there! I was accepted at Agnes Scott College in Atlanta. It had come about rather casually in the course of a morning's conversation.

An alumna of Agnes Scott, whom Mother admired, had praised the college highly and had offered to recommend me, and Mother had suddenly remembered, "Oh, yes! That's where they were so nice to Alice! It will be just the place." Her younger sister Alice, who had lived with us while attending the university, had before her marriage served Agnes Scott briefly as a librarian. Alice was no longer there, however, and I would be alone among strangers. I was not quite sixteen.

As passionately as I had once clung to my dolls in the old playroom, I now clung to my friends in the Comus Club. The summer days passed in a flurry of college preparations sandwiched between picnics, swimming parties and camping trips. Then in August I began a mournful countdown: this is the last club meeting, the last party, the last swim. I wondered if my friends knew how much I loved them all. I couldn't bear the thought that I would be replaced in the circle, that all the fun would continue without me, and I wouldn't be missed at all.

I had reckoned without the warm-hearted ingenuity of the Comuses, who were planning a send-off affair for me beyond anything I could have dreamed. Again it was Hermione, the gay little chatterbox, who had the idea and who somehow managed to inveigle me to her house all unsuspecting on the night before my journey. There they were—all eight of them—and on the table was a giant cake, "Goodbye, Helen" lettered in the icing. I could scarcely see the girls' faces through my tears, but there was more to come. Mary handed me a small package, tightly sealed. "We've all written letters to say goodbye, but you must cross your heart and promise you won't read them until you're on the train!" I solemnly swore and kissed them all goodbye as I would leaving in the early morning long before any of the others were awake.

The dingy railroad station looked very forlorn in the gray morning light as the Negro porter hauled down my shiny wardrobe trunk from the back of the Buick. The great black engine was already snorting and puffing as it took on water, and the unforgettable smell of train dust and cinders revived in me the excitement of bygone trips to Grandma's home in Columbiana. Only this time I would be traveling alone. I threw my arms around Daddy and buried my face against his chest, then realized that Mother was saying, "I think there's somebody here to see you."

Yes! That unmistakeable explosion of rattles and honks could mean only one thing! I looked up and saw the two open flivvers with their painted legends "Excuse my dust" and "It shakes you up." Behind the steering wheels were the grinning faces of Diddle and Bo Mack as the Comuses spilled out around me, their hair half-combed and their eyes puffy from lack of sleep. My fears vanished as I was swept aboard the train in the midst of the Comuses' parting shouts of encouragement.

I waited a long time before I opened the box of train letters which was beside me on the dusty red plush seat. When I did read them, one by one, the warm aura of each familiar presence filled my mind: Mary's note, long and full of shared recollections; cute little Sarah Sims' letter, jolly and joking; popular Winkie's letter concerned about my shyness and giving me helpful advice about how to make friends; Sarah's note thanking me for little things I had done for everyone, all of which I believed had gone unnoticed. Hermione's letter surprised me with a thoughtfulness I had never suspected as she told me how much she had enjoyed planning the farewell party, but Mabel's letter was a revelation.

"You wouldn't believe how jealous of you I've always been," Mabel had written, "and it's only now when you're going away, that I realize how I really do love you." How strange life was. I remembered how miserable I had been during those interminable dances, looking longingly at Mabel's blond curls surrounded by would-be partners, And all the time she had been jealous of me!

It is well that we live each day innocent of its successors. As I sat in the stuffy car clasping my treasured box, I could never have believed that very soon these Comus Club days would shrink in memory like my childhood, that my mind would be filled with the college world of lectures and concerts, of soul-searching and concern for the problems of the real world, that some day I would even look back in wonder at how blindly smug and self-satisfied we all had been in our rose-tinted round of picnics and parties.

Of this awakening to come I was blissfully unaware as I read and reread my letters. I think I still have them tucked away somewhere among old wedding notes and outgrown baby shoes and other similar souvenirs of a busy life. I have never needed to look for them because I know them all by heart.

Chapter Nine

Seasoned Lightly with "Alabama Corn"

The large land sale which Daddy completed in 1923 had made us, by our small-town standards, quite rich. About the same time, other changes were at work in our town, and particularly in the university. We had always felt a tie with the university. Our neighborhood was full of professors, and one of Mother's younger brothers or sisters was always living with us while attending classes. Now the college girls were appearing in peek-a-boo blouses and silk stockings, their hair puffed out over wads called "rats" and it was whispered that the university was becoming "the home of the drunks." A student who lived on our street was put in the asylum, and another lost his eyesight from drinking "bathtub gin." Dancers went into ever stranger gyrations to the sounds of the new jazz.

But Mother gloried in every minute of that era!

Once, when a friend complimented her on the delicious Delmonico pudding which she still made on rare occasions, I heard her answer, "Well, it's supposed to be flavored with brandy, you know, but since Prohibition I season it lightly with Alabama corn!"

How I hated her cocktail parties! Mother's long skirts and wavy, light brown pompadour had given way to a boyish bob and she wore long-waisted dresses with very short skirts. I resented her predilection for bright colors and too-red lipstick, and I bristled when occasionally someone thought Mother was my older sister. I don't think Daddy particularly liked the parties either, though he never tired of dancing and seemed to enjoy the sophisticated repartee of the young professors whom Mother delighted in gathering for these occasions. I usually managed to avoid the house when a party was in progress, although once or twice an inebriated young man would try to draw me into a lopsided conversation.

I have a vague remembrance of the poet Clement Wood and his wife, both in rather high spirits. They had come from New York to visit his alma mater. I have a more vivid recollection of a whirlwind evening with Zelda and Scott Fitzgerald, an evening which ended with Zelda being carried away in the back seat of the Fitzgeralds' open car, her feet sticking out the window. It was shortly after this that I heard Mother express the fervent wish that she could stay young forever and that she would not mind dying before she was forty. When I reminded her of this many years later, however, she swore she had never said anything of the sort. Perhaps I heard amiss or, more likely, maybe Mother was in no state to remember making the remark.

Sadly, I must admit Mother was growing a little too fond of the drinking that was such a necessary adjunct to the gaiety. Daddy, who was naturally moderate in everything, would nurse one or two highballs through a long evening, but Mother was no more temperate in this than in any of her other pleasures. As a girl, her natural shyness had sometimes made conversation difficult for her, but as the keg-ripened Alabama "corn" began to flow, she would become the life of the party. Because Mother had been slightly deaf ever since a youthful ear infection, she was not aware of how loud and carrying her voice would get as she swirled among the dancers in her accordion-pleated skirts.

I can remember only one party which I enjoyed as a participant. I must have been about fifteen at the time, for the occasion was after the advent of the Charleston, a dance which put a premium on youth and which we enjoyed immensely at our teenage gatherings. Mother was determined to master that difficult new dance, so much so that she organized a Charleston instruction class. I couldn't help being amused at the perspiring efforts of her friends, many of them growing now a little stout and stiff in the joints. Then I was introduced to the dark, handsome instructor the ladies had hired. He was a football hero named Johnny Mack Brown, who would later rise to fame in the movies after leading the Crimson Tide to an immortal victory in the Rose Bowl. I was thrilled when Johnny Mack invited me to be his partner to demonstrate the complicated steps—although I knew it was only because I happened to be handy—and I couldn't help being a little sad when I learned that he was engaged to pretty Cornelia Foster, who played the violin in our church.

Undoubtedly Mother's gay parties brought her much criticism from the more staid members of society, probably more than she deserved. Hating the least show of hypocrisy, Mother boldly displayed her new life to all the social critics and, although Daddy may not always have approved, he continued to spoil and indulge her. Although they quarreled sometimes during those years, Mother noisily and Daddy trying to suffer grimly in silence, this apparently mismatched couple actually loved each other deeply, as different as they were.

One thing Mother and Daddy shared was the ability to form enduring friendships. Both were generous to a fault, and our home soon became a haven for various friends who were in trouble or who needed an understanding ear. Mother not only hated gossip but almost automatically would take the side of the underdog. Toward the end of her life, I heard a long-time friend say that in all the years she had known Laurie, she had never heard Laurie say an unkind word about anyone.

Some of the young professors who attended Mother's parties undoubtedly came only for the free drinks and the fun, but others who grew to know Mother better appreciated her keen mind and her intense desire for self improvement. One of these was Carl Carmer, an English instructor from upstate New York who was having marital troubles. He was a large, fair, and rather florid young man. Some years earlier he had married Doris, an older woman who worshiped him. Until I knew the kindness beneath Doris' unprepossessing exterior, the straight short hair and baggy clothes and heavy stockings which she affected, I wondered how on earth the handsome and magnetic Carl had ever happened to marry her. The gossips claimed he'd married Doris for her money, as she was said to be very rich.

I do remember one occasion when Carl exploded to Mother, "Dammit, I just can't take it any more! Nothing is ours! Everything is hers—her house, her furniture, her car, her dog . . ." This last item referred to a tangled-looking poodle, appropriately named Rags, that always accompanied her. Soon after Carl departed, refreshed by his outburst, Doris appeared at the door with a long face and plaintive voice.

"Has Carl been here by any chance, Laurie? It seems as though we always bring our troubles to you, but honestly I just don't know where else to turn. Nothing I do seems to please him . . ."

Carl's career at the university was comet-like. He inspired his pupils with his own burning love of poetry and drama, publishing the students' best work in hard covers and sponsoring a yearly musical comedy production featuring local talent in the latest Broadway hits. I danced in one of the choruses, although some of my friends' parents disliked Carl's explosive and intemperate language during his direction of our awkward maneuvers. Part of his trouble at the university stemmed from the coeds who persisted in falling in love with him, and some claimed this was not all one-sided. However that might be, he eventually resigned from both his job and his marriage, though never from Mother's friendship.

Many Tuscaloosans were outraged when Carl's *Stars Fell on Alabama* was published believing themselves to be caricatured or unfairly portrayed, but Mother remained loyal. A few years ago, when Mother was in her seventies, she had a long visit from Carl and his attractive second wife, Betty. He had returned to the South on assignment for *Holiday* magazine to write an article on "Alabama Revisited." Later, Ira Moody said to me, laughing, "I guess your mother and I are about the only friends Carl has left in Tuscaloosa, but I'll always feel he's one of the most attractive men I've ever known."

After Carl left Tuscaloosa, Doris again came to see Mother for advice. Mother's counsel was both practical and imaginative. She suggested that Doris go to Paris and put herself in the hands of professionals who could teach her how to wear her clothes and hair—become, in short, a new woman. The recipe worked so well that, some years later, a radiant Doris introduced us to her second husband, a handsome engineer five years younger than she with whom she was destined to spend many happy years in their new home on Mobile Bay.

Of all the members of the university group, however, Mother's most devoted friend throughout her life was Hudson Strode. He was first introduced at one of her parties as a young English instructor who had just arrived from Demopolis, Alabama, and was then boarding in the neighborhood. A devotee of astrology, Hudson discovered that he and Mother had the same birthday, and thereafter he never failed to send her a favorite book inscribed with a humorous and affectionate message on those occasions. In fact, when Daddy became aware of how greatly Mother admired Hudson's taste in literature, it solved one of Daddy's own problems.

Despite all his efforts, Daddy could never please Mother in the matter of gifts. The lingerie he chose was too elaborate, the dinner ring too ornate, but the crowning disaster was the purple satin lounging pyjamas. They were awful! Finally, Mother tactfully suggested that Daddy simply give Hudson the money each Christmas to select books. This happy arrangement, along with her book club memberships, soon supplied Mother with a fine library.

When Hudson married dainty Theresa Cory of Birmingham, whose high-piled coils of black hair always reminded me of an Asian princess, Mother was delighted, and soon Theresa, too, became an intimate friend. It was Theresa's mother, the aristocratic Mrs. Chappell Cory, who was largely responsible for restoring the White House of the Confederacy in Montgomery and who first interested Hudson in writing his definitive three-volume *Biography of Jefferson Davis*.

There were times when Mother had to defend Hudson and Theresa as she had the Carmers, though for different reasons. The Strodes had some ideas which were unusual, to say the least. For many years they refused to burden themselves with possessions, living modestly in a small furnished apartment, in order to be free to travel at a moment's notice. They preferred walking to owning a car and eschewed a radio in favor of books and magazines. Some tongues wagged when the Strodes joined the small Christian Science group that met in a local movie house. Yet it was the Strodes' deviations from the ordinary that endeared this couple to my mother, who always remained their fervent admirer.

One reason for Hudson's devotion to Mother was the loyal support and encouragement she gave him during the years of his forced retirement. He was a born teacher, particularly in the demanding field of creative writing, as the shelves full of books published by his former students testify. He brought Shakespeare to life for his classes by acting out the roles himself, and, in addition, he sometimes gave public recitals of his favorite plays. He welded the struggling Blackfriars into a dynamic group, often producing plays of the students' own composition. I remember seeing some of these performances, and they were quite professional. Unlike most members of the English department, Hudson refused to employ readers, preferring to give each student's work his personal attention. It is not surprising that all that activity led to a nervous collapse.

Forbidden by the doctor to do any work whatsoever, or even to use his eyes, Hudson and Theresa eventually decided to move to the mild climate and serene beauty of Bermuda where, in those days, one could live very cheaply. A packet of charming letters from Theresa described to Mother the quiet life in Bermuda and Hudson's slow recovery of his health. Fascinated by the history and legends of the island, he began to collect them into a book, with Theresa as his amanuensis, which would prove to be the first of a long series of delightful travel books. I have just been rereading Mother's copy of *The Story of Bermuda*, inscribed "To Laurie, with the love of the author, 1932." I believe Mother felt she had a personal share in that book.

By the time the Strodes returned to Tuscaloosa and the Carmers had departed, I was away at college in Atlanta, and the nation was on the eve of the Great Depression. Needless to say, the parties were suddenly terminated. Daddy, who had expected to live on the income from his gilt-edged investments, found his capital rapidly dwindling. I recall an argument between him and Mother over whether a friend in Birmingham had been justified in committing suicide when—as happened in this case—there was no suicide clause in his life insurance policy. Although he defended his friend on that occasion, Daddy himself managed to survive with his sense of humor intact. He made brave efforts to curb his natural extravagance and, on the whole, did fairly well, although we lived on borrowed money for years. Surprisingly, it was Mother's adaptability and her sturdy Longshore practicality which provided the balance wheel of our household in those trying times.

Mother had always been a little shocked by Daddy's cavalier attitude toward money—his open-handedness on trips, his generous tipping, his expensive gifts on numerous occasions. Her own childhood experience of doing without all except the essentials of food and clothing had not prepared her for Daddy's insistence, even during hard times, that she just charge everything she needed. "I'll see that it's taken care of, Honey!" Daddy had old-fashioned scruples about discussing business affairs with women. For many years after their marriage Mother actually had no accurate estimate of his income. She was in for a rude awakening when one day early in the Depression, Daddy came home with the rueful announcement that he had just had to sell a valuable business lot in the center of town for a fraction of its value in order to settle a debt.

Mother told me about it years later. "I cried all afternoon over his having to sell that lot. Then that night I just sat him down and made him tell me exactly how much we owed—right down to the penny. I made him show me all the bills and we went over them together . . . then we worked out a plan to live by."

I began to remember many small economies that had gone almost unnoticed at the time. The expensive array of party dresses had vanished along with the parties, and Mother had begun to wear her simple cotton golf dresses every day. Actually they were very becoming to her, and she had never really cared much for clothes. I recalled how Mammy's salary had been discontinued, and how Mother had begun to take over many household chores that once had required extra servants. The biggest change came, though, when Mother conceived the idea of using the big house as a source of income.

At first Daddy flatly refused to consider such a thing. I suppose the thought of it hurt his pride. However, as he had long been accustomed to the young Longshores staying with us while going to college, Mother eventually won his approval to her plan of building an apartment in the attic for unmarried Aunt Lallage when the government Veterans' Bureau for which she worked moved its offices to Tuscaloosa. Mother was in her element when she was supervising a building job. She had discovered a talented Negro carpenter named Ed Bouyer who could build almost anything if Mother showed him exactly how she wanted it to look. Soon Mother and Ed were spending long days in the dusty attic and the little apartment gradually took shape.

It was the failure of the bank of which Daddy was a director that brought us our first boarder in the form of an attractive bachelor, Billikin Verner, who had often made a fourth at the bridge table. He had been left homeless when his uncle, the former bank president, had been offered a position in Washington. We all enjoyed Billikin, who frequently contributed to our table venison and other game from his hunting expeditions. After Billikin left, there were others.

Being poor somehow did not seem so terrible when everyone else suffered the same predicament. In a way it was rather a relief no longer to live in the giddy, unnatural whirl of the twenties. After a little time, Daddy could say with a rueful smile, "Well, about all I got out of being rich was the money I spent—the house all fixed up, the new car, the trip to Canada. But it's not too bad to have all that to look back on, and we're better off than lots of other folks."

Chapter Ten

College Days—A World Without Boys

My freshman year at Agnes Scott College was a disaster. From the moment my taxi disgorged me on the brick walk in front of the austere square Gothic tower of Main Hall among a crowd of well-dressed girls and their dignified parents, I felt lonely, awkward, and out of place. My one slim hope lay in the roommate I was soon to meet.

Mother's young friend, Evelyn Wood, who had persuaded her to send me to Agnes Scott, had arranged for me to room with the younger sister of a former classmate. "Ditty's bound to be a honey if she's anything like Roberta, and she doesn't know a soul there either." Evelyn had reassured me.

Maybe Ditty won't like me, I worried as I set down my luggage in the bare, high-walled room on the second floor of Main Hall. The two upper floors housed the freshmen, conveniently near the administrative offices downstairs. But when Ditty came in, I liked her at first sight. She was a tall, graceful girl with shining eyes and long, beautiful hands. That made the blow even crueler, though, for she was not to be my roommate after all.

"I feel just awful about it, especially now that I've met you! But when I saw Gay on the train coming here—this girl I knew at camp last summer—she begged me to room with her. We've just been down to get permission. I am sorry, and I do hope you get somebody nice!"

The trouble was that most people were already paired off. I was a leftover. I was stuck with a last-minute arrival, a loud, boisterous girl with a wide mouth full of big teeth, a closet full of bright—colored clothes, and a victrola with all the latest hot tunes. Maggie's only conversational subjects were her clothes and her "boyfriends," and as I cared little about what I wore and had never had a boyfriend, she found me as big a bore as I found her.

In my efforts to escape Maggie and her noisy cohorts, I found refuge in the library—I was always at home with books. Sometimes, after the library closed, I would go up to the piano practice rooms in the attic of Main Hall. They were dark and empty at night, and I would stand at one of the small dormer windows looking down at the semicircle of lamp posts wreathed in mist under the big trees of the drive, watching the lighted streetcars in the distance. Sornetimes a train would rumble by, its lonesome whistle echoing my own misery.

Once or twice I phoned Mary, but her gay chatter about the old crowd and their doings made the distance between us even greater. I could not go back to that world, and I had not yet come to terms with my new one.

One morning a tall, dark-haired sophomore came to my door, her arms full of poster paper. "I'm Sally Sutherland," she announced brusquely. "It says here on my list that you like to draw."

I remembered the forms we had filled out on which we had to list our hobbies or talents. "I'm not much good at it," I ventured. "I've never had a lesson."

"If you can spare the time, I'll show you how. All you need is a ruler, India ink and lettering pens." Whereupon Sally spread her materials on the table and gave me a lesson in poster making. It was the first of hundreds of posters I would make during the next four years on every conceivable subject—basketball and hockey games, Y.W.C.A. meetings, exhibits, lectures. I was a glutton for punishment, but the work filled many an empty hour and I gradually acquired skill and ingenuity.

At first, though, I made a few "boners," and Sally got a big laugh out of one of them. She had come rushing in to demand a poster in a big hurry. "Some girls have been ruining the clay tennis courts by playing in street shoes after a rain. I need to get this one up right away!"

My first effort read: "Please do not play on court when wet or in street shoes." That didn't sound right! I'd have to do it over. I used the back side and started again: "Please do not play when court is wet or in street shoes." Damn! I'd have to go to Sally and get more paper. From then on I took my time and got my poster planned out before I began.

Indirectly the poster making led me into another field. I became a scenery designer. The big event of the freshman year was the freshman-sophomore "stunt"—an original, vaudeville-type stage competition that drew a large audience from Decatur and even from Atlanta. I was thrilled when a group of my classmates asked me to design the stage sets, though I had no idea how to begin.

"It's new to all of us," said Chopin, one of the group. "But if you can come up with good ideas for posters, you ought to be able to do scenery. We've got to have something really original to win the Black Cat for our class!" Chopin—her full name was Anne Chapin Hudson was a small, energetic girl with bright dark eyes in a deeply tanned face. She excelled in sports and was a born leader. As we worked together on our "stunt," which was a rousing success, I found out that she was also warm and kindhearted.

"I've noticed you don't fit in with your roommate's crowd," she told me one day. "Why don't you come up and spend the night with us?"

That was the first of many visits to the big, hospitable corner room that Chopin shared with two girls who had been at boarding school with her the year before. I was in for a surprise, though, when something waked me in the middle of the night. Chopin was tossing and muttering in her sleep. Then the words became clearer, but I still could not understand them. Suddenly I realized—she was talking in Chinese! Next morning Chopin explained that she had grown up in China, where her father was a missionary, and had learned Chinese from her nurse.

Agnes Scott gave special rates to daughters of Presbyterian missionaries and preachers, so we had a great many of them. One girl told me that she got her first "bought" clothes when she came away to school. She had always had to make do with the cast off garments from the missionary barrels.

One of Chopin's roommates, Julia Thompson, was a preacher's daughter from Richmond, Virginia. I would meet her distinguished father three years later when he came to deliver our graduation sermon. Julia had a round face and short brown wavy hair. She shared with me the distinction of being the youngest of our class, having just turned sixteen. At first I thought Julia's accent sounded affected, as she had a rather precise way of talking and used the broad 'a' for certain words. I changed my mind after a little scene I witnessed one afternoon.

As I came to the door of their room, a girl from across the hall was saying teasingly to Julia, "If you're going to use the broad 'a' for 'half'—she drawled the word out exaggeratedly—then you ought to say 'pahst.' Why don't you say them both alike?"

Julia's face was fiery red and she seemed on the verge of tears. "I can't help the way I talk." she almost screamed. "All my family, everybody I *know* at home talks like I do! I think you're mean, all of you!" She covered her face in embarrassment, and it took some time to pacify her. After that I never felt again that Julia was standoffish.

It was the third roommate, Weesa Chandler, whose father was a navy officer in Washington, D.C., who became my closest friend. She was in my class in English composition, and one day our teacher read aloud a theme I had written. As we left the room, Weesa said to me with a glowing face, "I'd give anything in the world if I could write like that!" Weesa was not a writer, but she was that rarest of all things, a wonderful appreciator. One day I found her huddled up in bed with a book across her knees, sobbing her eyes out.

"What's the matter, Weesa? What in the world has happened?" I asked in alarm, thinking she must have had bad news from home.

"Cyrano's dead!" she sobbed. Cyrano de Bergerac! "Oh, it's so sad, but it's so beautiful!"

Everything about Weesa was wholehearted and unrestrained. She had a pretty face under an untidy mop of brown curls and a soft, bosomy figure. She was sensitive, sentimental, forgetful, and generous. Her speaking voice was so rich and melodious that it was a shame she was completely tone deaf. She might have made a great singer.

When I went home for the Christmas holidays, Mother surprised me with a party to which she had invited all my old crowd. There was even a date for me with Philip, the boy next door, who had always been one of my few male admirers. In fact, he had been the first boy I ever dated, an occasion that I would never forget.

Half-paralyzed with shyness and searching frantically for something to talk about, I had begun gabbling about my recent attempts at sculpture in clay. I had just modelled the head of a small boy, and I gestured toward it proudly, remarking, "By the way, have you seen my bust?"

"No, but I'd like to," replied Philip.

We laugh over it now, but it was not funny to me at the time!

It was good to see my friends again, but I began to realize that in some indefinable way I was growing away from them. I suppose some of the churchy atmosphere of Agnes Scott was rubbing off on me. An incurable idealist, I had even attended one meeting of the Future Missionary Society and had formed a vague picture of myself healing the starving babies in some far-off part of the world. Anyway, for whatever reason, my new serious self found my high school friends rather young and sometimes, yes, even silly.

The big finale of the holidays at that time in Tuscaloosa was the Warrior Guard dance on New Years Eve, given annually by our local company of National Guards which included most of the nicest young men in town. I wanted very much to go. Dancing with boys was forbidden at Agnes Scott—we danced only with each other. But to attend this affair would have made me miss a day of school which entailed a strict penalty. Daddy said jokingly, "Well, the only way you could make it would be to fly back to Atlanta on the mail plane!"

Airplane flights were a very new thing in 1928, and it was only recently that a small four-passenger plane had begun to fly the mail from a converted pasture outside Northport. I knew Daddy was not serious—but I was. I was eager to fly, and I could usually wheedle what I wanted from Daddy. I stayed for the dance and went back to college in style, only it turned out to be even greater style than I had bargained for.

The mail plane landed me safely at the Atlanta airport, a small wooden building miles from town and surrounded by empty fields. There were two cars outside, but one of them pulled away just as we arrived. I had shared the last part of the plane ride with one other passenger, a distinguished-looking middle-aged gentleman. He started toward the other car, a long black limosine, then turned back to me. "Young lady, it looks like you'll have to share my car. I'd be pleased to take you to your destination."

"I'm going back to Agnes Scott College. It's pretty far," I told him doubtfully.

Just then a uniformed chauffeur came out of the building and was told to detour by way of Decatur. During the ten mile ride the obliging stranger introduced himself. He was the president of the airline!

Toward the end of the spring term people began choosing roommates for the next year. Finally I nerved myself to ask Weesa, as I knew the trio had decided to separate. Unfortunately, I had waited too long. Weesa had already agreed to room with a junior girl whose roommate was leaving school.

"I'd rather roorn with you," Weesa told me regretfully, "but I felt sorry for her and I can't back out now."

"No you mustn't do that," I said, remembering my own earlier experience with Ditty.

A few days later, however, Weesa and Chopin found me a roommate, one of the missionary's daughters with whom I had a slight acquaintance. She was a quiet, shy girl and a straight 'A' student. I looked forward with relief to the end of the hot music and the dirty jokes.

Poor Maggie! She and one of her wilder friends were expelled from school early in the sophomore year. It seems she had hidden a car off-campus—cars were forbidden, of course—and had been caught spending evenings at Georgia Tech fraternity houses. It was even rumored that they drank! When these reports were whispered to us, we stared at each other and shook our heads sadly.

My own fate was almost as bad, however. My sweet little

sophomore roommate developed a schoolgirl crush on a husky-voiced, aggressive girl who soon became a permanent presence in our room. My only retreat was the bathroom. One night Jean Gray found me there, trying to study in the glaring light over the washbasins. "I know what's going on down there," Jean said with an understanding gleam in her blue eyes. "Come on down to our room when it gets too bad. Dell and I will understand."

I was glad to find sympathy without having to say anything, feeling vaguely that it was the sort of thing one shouldn't talk about. I realize now that these adolescent crushes were inevitable in the restricted, unnatural atmosphere of our boyless world. Both those girls are happily married now, with successful careers and grown families.

Jean Gray had more daring than I. One day in our psychology class she asked right out loud if there was anything abnormal about girls falling in love with other girls. The teacher hemmed and hawed and finally gave an evasive answer, so we remained mystified. Jean winked at me and shrugged her shoulders.

How innocent we were! I knew there were boys who were sissy and girls who went around hugging each other, but I had been out of college for years before I knew about words like homosexual or lesbian or gay. Our thoughts mainly centered around studies, or sports, or the host of other activities offered on the campus.

I went in big for clubs that year, partly as an escape from my invaded room. I tried out for everything that I had a chance of getting into: dramatic club—for scenery designing, of course—poetry club, magazine staff, and swimming and water polo teams. There was not much time left to worry about questions that seemed to have no answer.

I even taught a colored Sunday school class occasionally and was co-leader with Weesa for a Girl Scout troop at a local junior high. Once or twice some of us were persuaded by our Young Women's

Christian Association director to join an interracial forum in an Atlanta church that was led by Dr. Eleazar and included Negro students from Morehouse College. It was a very daring thing to do in those days and a little frightening, as we had an uncomfortable feeling that our parents would definitely not have approved.

When I became a junior I acquired a freshman "little sister," Vivian Martin, from Ann Arbor, Michigan, whom I was supposed to help and guide in her adjustment to the school. As it turned out, my friendship with Vivian gave me a new and broader view of the racial problem. She was a cute little round—faced girl with a head full of short brown ringlets, and on my first visit I found her in the throes of homesickness, her eyes red from crying.

"I know I'm going to like it here." She sniffled and tried to smile. "It's just . . . you caught me when I was missing my mother. She died two years ago—we were so close—and I don't like my new stepmother and her crowd at all. That's one reason I came down South, to get away from her and to be near my grandparents in Atlanta."

"How nice that your grandparents live here," I said consolingly, already won over by Vivian's appealing manner. "I'd love to meet them sometimes."

"They're wonderful people, but I don't know whether you'd want to meet them," said Vivian doubtfully. "You see, they teach in a Negro college, Gammon Seminary . . . and they *live* there!"

"Why, I think that's a fine thing for them to do. I admire them for it." Then I added, feeling proud of it for the first time, "Anyway, I've been going to the Interracial Forum in Atlanta."

Vivian's face cleared. "Have you really? Then perhaps you would like to visit them. You know, my grandparents have been here for years, and in all that time not a single white Southern woman has visited my grandmother. She loves people, so I know she gets lonely sometimes."

I soon discovered that Vivian and I not only shared a love for books and writing—she wrote charming little essays—but we both enjoyed taking long walks along the quiet, tree-lined residential streets of Decatur. I had made the swimming and water polo teams and was working toward my letter in athletics. When I found out that I could acquire the requisite number of points by taking ten-mile hikes, I proposed to Vivian one day that we walk the ten miles out to Gammon Seminary on Sunday and visit her grandparents. We could come back to school early Monday morning on the streetcar.

Vivian was enthusiastic, so we went to the Dean's office to get permission. Miss Nanette Hopkins was a tiny, exquisite lady from Virginia who wore her hair in a snowy old-fashioned pompadour. One of the greatest honors that could come to a senior was to win the Anette Hopkins Medal for coming the nearest to her ideal of a perfect lady. She seemed as fragile as a Japanese teacup but actually she was quite strict.

"So you want to walk all that way?" she questioned us in her soft voice. "Well, I suppose it's all right. But, girls," she leaned forward, "there's just one thing. If I were you, I wouldn't go through any *disreputable* sections!"

We kept our faces straight until we were safely outside. Then we doubled up with laughter. It was such a typical remark. All the way to Gammon Seminary on Sunday, as we walked past monotonous rows of suburban cottages and through sprawling Negro slums, we would grin at each other and ask, "Wonder if she'd think this section was disreputable." It added a bit of spice to the long walk.

Once we arrived, though, the visit was well worth the effort. As I looked at those two serene and saintly-looking old faces, I wondered how it could be possible to feel anything but awed respect for their years of work and sacrifice. The Spartan simplicity of the small cottage on the leafy campus, the bareness of the refrigerator—we had a tiny piece of ham, one potato, and a baked apple for supper—all spoke of life at a bare subsistence level.

Vivian's grandfather, obviously eager for understanding from a white Southerner, explained carefully that his aim was not social integration. "We want vertical integration, not horizontal," he aaid earnestly, "just a chance for each human being to grow upward as far as he is able."

After supper we walked across the campus in the dusk towards the lighted chapel from which we already heard the muted harmony of blended voices. Just as we sat down in the back row, a Negro girl with a high, sweet voice stood and sang a line which the others answered in chorus. Then another singer rose and was answered in turn.

"They make up the songs as they go along, just like the old-time spirituals," Mr. Martin whispered. "We're trying to teach them to take pride in their own heritage rather than imitating the music of the white man."

When I listened to that glorious outpouring of music and watched the utter absorption in those upturned faces, I felt a glimmer of understanding of why this couple had chosen to devote their lives to this far-off corner of the South.

I had begun my junior year in a single room. I wanted no more roommates. There were a few two-story clapboard cottages on campus where only upperclassmen were permitted to live. It was the nearest thing to a sorority that the college offered, and I rather looked forward to living in one of them with a group of my friends. However, I did not even have time to get acquainted with my new room. About the end of the first week, Mary Terry, a senior whom I knew from Latin class, came to me with an urgent request.

"I know you don't know me very well," she said, "but I think we've enough in common to get along together. The thing is, I *have* to have a roommate. I've been made president of Inman Hall, which puts me on the Student Council, but it's required that I have a roommate who will automatically be the vice-president. You'd be my substitute on student council, too, and could go if you liked. Please say you will!"

I studied Mary while I thought about it. She had a long, serious face, straight hair, and an awkward, striding walk with her head thrust forward. She was from a small country town in Alabama and wore shapeless cotton dresses that always seemed to sag at the hem. Her one beauty was her big expressive brown eyes which were now shining with eagerness. I felt that this position meant a great deal to her, and after all, what did I have to lose?

"Okay," I said finally. "I chose to room by myself mainly because I wanted a quiet place to study."

"I promise I won't get in your hair, and I need to pull my grades up, too," she said.

I decided Mary was almost pretty when she smiled, and I never regretted my decision to room with her. She was a restful person, the kind people gravitated to when they were in trouble. She mothered all the misfits in the dormitory and was especially good with homesick freshmen. She was so grateful to me, too, and had such a high opinion of me that it boosted my often lagging self-confidence.

Weesa had been made head of the campus lecture association, which invited important personages to the school. Once or twice I went with her to meet and welcome these guests. There was the Socialist, Norman Thomas, with his gentle, scholarly face, not at all the villain I had been led to expect by the newspapers. Carl Sandberg played his guitar and sang folk songs for us. I remember his definition of poetry: "It's a pink balloon filled with gas that is pulled toward the sky but is held to earth by a string clutched in a child's hand." There was Thornton Wilder, handsome and young-looking, who caused a stir of excitement among the girls. We were even more thrilled over the virile and good-looking hero of the day, Admiral Richard Byrd, who had just returned from the Antarctic.

The most personally moving experience for me was meeting Robert Frost on the first of his many visits to Agnes Scott. He had long been in correspondence with my favorite English teacher, Miss Emma Mae Laney. She was a scrawny, ugly woman with a rasping voice and a passion for beautiful language which she somehow succeeded in passing along to her pupils. One of them said later, in tribute, "She drew out of us what we did not know we had in us." She had also embued us with a great admiration for Frost, whom she was one of the first to recognize as a master poet. And, of course, he charmed us all.

During my senior year I helped in promoting a love affair, which was the next best thing to having one. After a few sad experiences with blind dates, in which we sat rigidly in the Main Hall date parlors under the eyes of a matron and inquisitive passing freshmen, I had just about decided to put off thinking about boys until summer. But Shirley McPhaul was already engaged to Randy Whitfield, a graduate engineering student at Georgia Tech. All of us loved Shirley who was a warm, friendly girl with auburn hair, a sprinkling of freckles, and an infectious laugh. She was elected editor of the annual and chose me as her art editor. A calamity threw us together.

The Great Depression which swept across the country in 1930 had its repercussions on our campus, of course, but it did not really hit us directly until the local Decatur bank failed. It carried with it the four thousand dollars set aside to publish the *Silhouette*, our college annual. Shirley called a staff meeting to announce the sad news. "I guess it means we can't have an annual this year. The bank plans to pay off about one-fourth, I think, but that's not nearly enough."

We sat in silence, digesting this news. Finally I asked, "What makes it cost so much? Four thousand dollars seems a lot to me."

"Well, last year the art work alone cost two thousand," answered Shirley. "I've just been studying the figures. There's all that engraving and professional art work for the different sections."

"Listen, Shirley, "I said in sudden excitement? "I'm no artist, but we've got plenty of talent in this school. Why can't we do our own art work—pen and inks instead of color, and drawings instead of fancy engravings. At least we'd be original!"

I had no idea what I was letting myself in for, but I soon learned. I found the six talented girls for my staff, but getting the work out of them was something else. I consulted with Shirley and the printers, then I pleaded, cajoled, and browbeat my artists to little avail. Though some good work came in very late, I ended up doing a large part of it myself, working until "lights out," then doing my schoolwork by flashlight.

I had decided to room alone, as my grades really needed attention. I was a lopsided student, good in English and history, but impossible in math, poor in French, and weak in sciences. In this crisis of the school annual, however, an attractive transfer student from Tennessee named Polly Cawthorn came to my rescue. She had a single room next door to mine, and she generously proposed that I move my bed into her room so that my own could be used as an art studio. Polly also became my model. Our annual was to carry out the theme of literature through the ages, and poor Polly would be draped in shawls or bedspreads to represent, in turn, Bede the Anglo-Saxon, Chaucer, or Shakespeare. Eventually I boldly ignored the "lights out" and worked far into the night, praying I would not fall asleep in class the next day.

Meanwhile, I was playing Cupid in Shirley's love affair. So much of our time at the printer's was connected with the art work that Shirley began leaving me there to finish up while she slipped out to meet Randy. Knowing how much it meant to them to be together, I finally suggested, "Shirley, why don't you give me a list of things you want done and let me handle it so you can spend more time with Randy?" So that was what we did—and we put out an annual that won first place in the regional competition.

Meanwhile, I somehow found enough spare time to put together the scenery for our "senior opera," another Agnes Scott traditional production. I worked closely on this with a brilliant and unusual girl named Ellene Winn, who had a single room on my hall. Our opera, a hilarious spoof called "O-hello," was her brainchild.

Ellene was a tall, angular girl with straight black hair drawn into a knot, a long sallow face and bright black eyes. As editor of the *Aurora*, our college magazine, she had often visited me to persuade me to turn in poems or stories. She had a gift for slightly malicious satire, and our opera was a smash hit.

I came to know Ellene well during those weeks. She talked about her big motherless family of brothers and sisters growing up in Clayton, Alabama—George Wallace's home town—and of how her father, the judge, brought them up on the Bible and Shakespeare. I learned about her crazy deaf aunt, kept in their home, who embarrassed the family by writing love letters to all the prominent men in town. Ellene claimed that her own penetrating, high-pitched voice was a result of having to shout at her aunt.

It shocked us all when Ellene, who practically knew the Bible by heart, received a 'B' in Bible Study. This course was taught by an iron-haired, stern-minded unmarried lady named Miss Pearl Sydenstricker, the aunt for whom Pearl Buck was named, and it was required for graduation. Under her we traced all the prophecies from Genesis through Revelations, and we gave the answers she expected—all of us, that is, except Ellene, whose mischevious demon made her persist in needling the poor woman with unanswerable questions. That 'B,' the only one she made, kept Elllene from earning the Phi Beta Kappa she richly deserved.

As for me, I never expected any honors, what with my low grades in math, so I went to chapel on Honors Day with a light heart, prepared to applaud for my more fortunate friends. When finally, toward the end of the occasion, the cap-and-gowned Mortar Board members came to the stage, the school leaders like Chopin and Shirley and the rest, I had not the faintest premonition. I had not even known any new members would be picked. When Chopin walked down the long aisle and tapped me on the shoulder, I looked up at her in bewilderment with my mouth dropped open. "Get up, you idiot," she whispered. "You're in Mortar Board!"

I remember walking across the campus by myself that night in the misty rain, trying to take it in. I had never been especially popular, had never been elected to any office. I had worked hard at first because I was lonely and had kept on because I had come to enjoy it. This was the first really big thing that had ever happened to me, and I somehow knew then that no later honor would ever have quite the same impact. Life was unpredictable, I thought, and, sometimes, very wonderful.

During that last college Spring, some of us began to worry about our future. As Chopin put it, "We know a lot, but what can we really do?" She meant, as she went on to explain, "What kind of jobs are we equipped for that will earn us any money?"

When we had thoroughly hashed over this topic, we regretfully agreed that none of us had any skills that people would pay us for in the dismal job market of the Depression. Agnes Scott offered no commercial courses, no teacher training. So we decided we would hire a business school teacher on our own who would come out to Agnes Scott and teach us to type.

Chopin, always practical, made the arrangements. We pooled our allowances, found a teacher, and rented four typewriters which the eight of us would take turns using. These were set up in some unused piano practice rooms in the attic, where our clacking typewriter keys soon vied with the scales and arpeggios. After a few basic lessons, our teacher told us we didn't need her any more—we only needed to practice. Most of us would be grateful for that improvised business school in the black days of job-hunting that lay ahead of us.

Most of us sensed, I think, that our college world was unreal, a sort of waiting period. The really big things—jobs, marriage, children, all that—were outside in that real world that seemed vaguely threatening as it drew closer. I had come to terms with Agnes Scott, though, and I found, somewhat to my surprise, that I rather dreaded leaving.

When finally the last day came, then the last night, with my room stripped and my clothes and books packed away, I went down to my "art studio" retreat, locked the door, and sat up far into the night trying to put it all into a poem. I called it "On Leaving College."

> One last remembering, one minute more,
> One glance around my room, then break the spell
> And pack away my books. No use to dwell
> On winged hours passing. Other girls before
> Have said good-bye and softly closed the door,
> Have looked down from this window, seen the swell
> And fading out of sunsets, loved as well
> As I the feel of misty nights, the muffled roar
> Of trains through darkness.   Future days I know
> Will hold as much of beauty. Come! Strip bare

The shelves and tables. What's an ended year
With all of life before me? Bravely go
Along the empty halls, nor turn to stare
At ghosts of days, dear days, behind me here.

I gave a copy to Weesa next day as a good-bye present. Some years later, in 1936, with my young husband and me almost broke and a car payment due, I would send it to *Good Housekeeping* where it would be published, the first piece of writing for which I ever received a check.

I meant every word of that poem. It expressed my mood at the time. But I have never been one for much looking back. In my secret heart I wished, like Thoreau, "to live deep and suck all the marrow out of life." It was time for me to leave the sheltering brick walls of this world without boys. I was ready for the next thing.

Chapter Eleven

They Called Him Singing Sam

My father was forty when he married, and I was born a year later. Accordingly, most of my impressions of his bachelor years in the "Gay Nineties" I have drawn from faded pictures in old albums and from his own delightful stories. He had a great fund of humorous anecdotes which lost none of their effect in the retelling and often, toward the end of the evening meal while the cook was clearing the table, we'd beg him to retell one of our favorites. My mother, who unfortunately lacked Daddy's sense of humor, would sometimes say plaintively, "But, Sam, are you sure it happened that way? Last time you said . . ."

"Now, Laurie," Daddy would moan in mock dismay, "it's *my* story: doesn't anybody want to hear it?"

"*Please* tell it, Daddy," we would all chorus eagerly, edging our chairs nearer to his place, and my mother's faint protest went unheeded. As I look back on those days of more than forty years ago, I can understand my mother's occasional lack of enthusiasm. She was twenty years younger than my father and the people and events in his stories were far out of her ken. Yet to the four of us children, his tales held absorbing interest.

I have long ago forgotten the details, but one favorite concerned a white-faced cow which, looming up on the dark country road in front of my father's buggy, unwittingly frightened a reluctant young maiden into his arms. Another anecdote recounted the time he had been visiting rich friends in New Orleans and had been showing off his horsemanship in the park. In the act of turning in the saddle to bow to a lovely equestrienne, he was struck unceremoniously in the stomach by a low tree branch and left hanging ingloriously in mid air. The tales themselves, of course, are nothing without the teller, his personality, and his consummate sense of drama. How he gloried in his art.

In the last year of my father's life, when he was eighty-one, the editor of our daily newspaper persuaded Daddy to record some of his early recollections, and our fellow townspeople were soon laughing with us at "Mr. Sam's" column.

In an editorial, the editor paid a glowing tribute to my father as "one of the city's true gentlemen," and one who "helped to bring about progress and to develop our great natural resources." I liked best the simple affirmation of Daddy's point of view: "He loved life and people. He was the kind of gentleman who would never knowingly run the risk of offending anyone if he could possibly avoid doing so . . . Tuscaloosa, to him, was a living community of warm, real people. He loved our city in that way . . . His wide circle of friends will treasure the memory of one who enriched the days of all around him."

Daddy's published reminiscences began when he was watching, at the age of six, a Japanese lantern parade commemorating the supposed inauguration of Samuel J. Tilden to the Presidency. News traveled so slowly in those days that it was two weeks before the citizens discovered that Rutherford B. Hayes had won the election.

The picture Daddy drew of the town in the decades following the Civil War was of "an aristocratic, nonprogressive town of slightly less than 2,000 people whose main idea seems to have been to keep the carpetbaggers and the Negro from infringing on their rights and privileges." He described the stern paddlewheelers on the river, the volunteer water bucket fire brigade, the old wagon trains crowded with farm folk who used to build their bonfires around the free whiskey barrel outside his father's store, and the old private schools, one of which he had attended until he entered the University of Alabama at the age of fourteen.

I still have the gold medal Daddy won "for declamation" at this small school conducted by Bishop Fonsdale in the Episcopal Church, and I also have a copy of Daddy's flowery speech in praise of Jefferson Davis, complete with gestures such as, "Put hand on heart here." Even then Daddy had delighted in entertaining an audience. He told us that once he had substituted for the juvenile lead when a troupe of actors had put on a performance in our town. He had felt quite heartbroken when his father had refused to let him join the company.

All his life Daddy cherished a frustrated dream of becoming an actor, and he rarely missed a good performance at the theater or the movies. He took us to all the various attractions which came to town—I particularly remember his enjoyment of "The Barber of Seville," "Rose Marie," and "Blossom Time"—and encouraged us to take part in the American Legion Follies, the latter put on with local talent by Carl Carmer.

Daddy organized a group of businessman to open the first movie theater in town and, as we all received free tickets, we seldom missed a movie. Daddy's favorite star was Will Rogers, whom Daddy much resembled in both manner and appearance, though not in ungrammatical diction. Once, after seeing Will Rogers play a country doctor role, Daddy remarked wistfully—he have been about seventy then—"You know, I believe I could play a character part like that, even now . . ."

Daddy loved dancing and in his youth was in great demand as a leader of "Germans" and polkas. One day in an old trunk I found a moth-eaten pennant inscribed with the letters L. T. F. This launched Daddy on a description of a once-illustrious group of wealthy young dandies whose sole function seems to have been organizing and giving an elaborate annual ball. I remember a picture of three girls wearing enormous hats tied with veils posed stiffly in my father's open touring car, one of the first in town. In his flowing script, Daddy had inscribed the picture "Dimples, Dottie, and Huylers," the last nickname, he explained, from the brand of candies she favored. These beauties had dared the hazardous sixty-mile auto tour from Birmingham to attend the L. T. F. Ball.

At the less glamorous country club dances I occasionally attended with my parents, I noticed a trait that partly explained Daddy's popularity with the female sex of all ages. He would almost invariably select for his partner someone sitting along the wall. I recall one gray-haired matron who exclaimed half-reluctantly, "Why, Sam, I can't dance. I've forgotten how! It's been so long!" Daddy was persuasive and, in no time at all, the elderly lady was swooping and gliding to the waltz he loved.

We teenagers preferred "break-in" dancing, as our peers as well as society frowned on "going steady," and a test of a girl's popularity was the number of boys who would tap the shoulder of her dancing partner. I can remember the grateful glances of many a young girl whom my kindhearted father rescued—myself among them—from the direful ignominy of being "stuck" with her date. Daddy's strong, gliding steps were easy to follow and he could make a shy partner appear so graceful and at ease that the reluctant swains would cut in again.

Among my newspaper clippings there are a few which describe my father as "Singing Sam," a nickname earned by his song-leading for the local Rotary Club which he had helped to found. He had a strong and melodious though untrained tenor voice, and gloomy was the day when he didn't come singing down the stairs to breakfast. The memory makes me shudder even now, as I was never a cheerful riser! His mother had been an accomplished pianist, and Daddy had composed a rolicking piano ditty at the age of four with which he sometimes favored us on happy occasions. He wished that he had not refused to take piano lessons, believing them to be "be sissy," and then he longed to find musical talent among his offspring, which hope, unfortunately, we never fulfilled. I suppose none of us who knew him will ever hear "My Wild Irish Rose" or "Down by the Old Mill Stream" without recalling Daddy, for those were his favorites. Everyone had to join the harmony, even the smallest grandchild, and the happiest times of all were those in his later years when our scattered brood gathered for summer vacations at "Dogwood Lodge."

This was a huge log cabin our parents had built in the pine-covered hills along a tumbling creek, and where the family lived every summer for fifteen years. My father dearly loved wandering in those woods, always carrying his tree pruners in case he encountered some young dogwoods or redbud trees to free from the entangling vines.

Daddy's father, Bernard, a Jew by birth though professing no particular religion, had come to the South in the 1850s as a young immigrant peddler from Hungary. The legend said that he had walked from New York to Georgia with his pack on his shoulders, soon exchanging the pack for a wheelbarrow, the wheelbarrow for a wagon, and finally, the wagon for a store. Bernard had settled in Tuscaloosa County because he foresaw a great future in its undeveloped mineral resources, especially iron ore and coal, and had gradually accumulated vast tracts of land which my father managed as an estate.

Daddy loved every foot of that land and grieved whenever he

had to cut a tree. He studied its forest and mineral resources, always dreaming he would strike oil some day. If mineral riches ever are found in this region, the benefactors of that event will owe some tribute to the vision of these two men, whose predictions often fell on deaf ears.

Daddy's more practical brother, my Uncle Hugo, considered over-optimism to be Daddy's greatest fault, and perhaps it was. Daddy ended his life in debt, primarily as a result of losses in the Depression. He had even sacrificed his life insurance in an effort to hold onto the land. Uncle Hugo helped Daddy out of many tight spots and, at his death, generously cancelled the debt still outstanding.

No greater contrast could have been found than the personalities of those two brothers who nevertheless held a deep affection for each other. Uncle Hugo, a well-to-do cotton broker and a lifetime supporter of the University of Alabama football team, was one of the great sportsmen of the area. Daddy, on the other hand, rarely caught a fish and never bagged a deer. Moreover, he was an unpopular companion on overnight outings because of his ungodly snore, which resembled the roar of a mountain lion and would have frightened away all the game animals. I sometimes wonder how my mother endured it.

By nature Daddy was a gambler, and this might have become his worst vice except for an incident that took place on his honeymoon, a grand tour of Europe. My youthful mother, having grown up in the church-centered home of a country judge with twelve children, enjoyed that new experience with excited wonder—that is, until she and Daddy reached Paris. There, my venturesome father made the acquaintance of some professional card sharks who promptly "took him to the cleaners."

Mother, meanwhile, had been left with some shipboard acquaintances at the hotel. When the time came for Mother's friends to retire, Daddy had still not returned. Frozen with fear, she sat on the bed in the strange hotel room until the small hours of the morning. Finally my defeated father arrived, put his arm around her and confessed the full extent of the calamity. "Honey," he said, "I've lost fifteen hundred dollars! Everything I own except our return tickets!"

Thus did my father learn a lesson about gambling, and thus did my mother learn the weakness of her new husband. Accustomed as she was to counting every penny, it was some months before she fully recovered from the shock. Daddy's banker wired them money enough to continue their tour, but on my father's return he was compelled to pay the piper. Until the borrowed money was reimbursed in full, he had to work out his debt in his father's department store, a job Daddy detested. It must have been a great relief to my father to finally sell the confining store. He simply didn't have a merchant's soul. Money, to him, was something one used for the greater enjoyment of life, in which latter pursuit he was quite successful.

Daddy never really gambled again, but he did instigate a pleasant nightly poker game at our country club during his later years. The game lasted exactly one hour, beginning at six, and the involvement of each man was limited to a "dollar a corner." On the stroke of seven, the winner pocketed the money. Thus did my father sublimate his dangerous urge. Like Benjamin Franklin, whose autobiography had much influenced him in boyhood, Daddy came to admire moderation above all other virtues except kindness.

Daddy also practiced moderation in drinking. It was his custom to have one "highball" each evening before dinner and never more than one except on the rarest occasions. Another regular habit was drinking a tall glass of sauerkraut juice in the morning before breakfast. He tried to promote the medicinal qualities of this beverage to the rest of the family, but we held our noses.

That custom, however, led to an amusing incident. When Billikin was staying with us, Mother called from the upstairs hall late one afternoon. "Billikin, go to the icebox and drink Sam's highball while you're waiting. I'll be down in a minute to fix him another." Shortly thereafter we all heard gagging sounds and a noise like a muffled explosion.

"Good Lord, Laurie, what *was* that stuff?" Billikin cried, emerging from around the kitchen door. At the same instant we realized the mixup and roared with laughter, all, that is, except Billikin.

Most days Daddy could be found in his office in his old swivel chair sagged backwards and his feet propped on an open drawer. Daddy said that he always did his best thinking in a semi-reclining position. Occasionally, he took off an afternoon for golf but usually he would be dictating to Miss Lena, his treasured longtime secretary, or swapping stories with one of his frequent visitors. I suppose the history of our town's progress could be traced in the record of those visitors—gangling country farmers, small mine operators, promoters, Negroes in trouble—they all invariably came to "Marse Sam." There were always businessmen, too, who simply enjoyed a good talk and went away refreshed.

When I was a child, Daddy's office held a great attraction for me. Although only a block from the center of town, the place was an odd choice for an office, being actually a dilapidated-looking, unpainted four-room house with an open center hall. A bench on the sagging front porch used to be occupied on good days by "Uncle Lige" Moore, who died when I was in my teens. This illiterate backwoodsman's tobacco-stained handlebar whiskers and unkempt clothing belied his shrewd mind. He knew or was kin to almost every inhabitant on Daddy's far-flung estate and proved invaluable to Daddy on his frequent country visits. One of my greatest pleasures was to be allowed to accompany Daddy on one of those all-day excursions along the bumpy, winding hill roads.

I would ply "Uncle Lige" with eager questions about where the old stagecoach roads had been and which settlers' cabins were the oldest. His memory was phenomenal. He adored my father and, sitting there in the sun on his bench by the door, "Uncle Lige" looked somewhat like a droopy hound dog guarding his master's sanctum.

Daddy's office was his sanctum. In the main room, to the right of the door, he had removed a partition to make a spacious area centered by a potbellied stove. Along the walls were the great iron safe and the towering bookcases of ancient ledgers. He was a civil engineer by profession so there were huge maps and prints made and lettered by my father's neat hand in the small blueprint room at the back of the building. The heart of the main office was Daddy's big flat-topped desk, flanked by Miss Lena's smaller one, and her somewhat battered typewriter. As most of this furniture had formerly belonged to my grandfather, there was a timeless air of continuity there.

The favorite hunting ground for my younger brother and me was Daddy's museum, across the hall. There in big glass cases was a treasure house of mineral samples and fossils which Daddy had collected on his walks in the woods, each specimen with a carefully printed legend. This collection is now in the university museum, of which Daddy was a director. Finally, there was the storeroom, with dusty stacks of old books and papers. In the rear of the old house, beyond the blueprints that usually hung drying on the open back porch, was, unexpectedly, a small fruit and vegetable garden.

Daddy did not care for flowers particularly—that was Mother's domain—but what he wanted most from his garden patch he never obtained. That was a horseradish as big as a man's head, a feat which Daddy vowed his father had once achieved. At any rate, the number and variety of Daddy's garden produce was amazing. There was a row of the white sweet corn he loved. There were tender pole beans, tomatoes, cantaloupes, and all sizes of cucumbers. At the very back of the patch, along the edge of the red clay gulley which the garden overhung, stood his beloved fruit trees. With the frequent gifts of melons and other items from his country friends, we never wanted for fresh fruit or vegetables and never knew what Daddy would bring home for dinner.

As he grew older, Daddy neglected his garden and kept shorter hours at the office, seeming to enjoy most his long discussions with congenial friends. When I was taking graduate courses at the university the last year I spent at home before my marriage, I grew very close to my father. Once or twice, to his great delight, I attended Ladies Day at his beloved Rotary Club. More frequently I would meet him for lunch at his favorite delicatessen, where we would invariably be joined by one or more of his friends.

My favorite participant at these "round table" discussions, as we dubbed them, was an elderly professor of philosophy and religion, Dr. Andy Lang, who was perhaps Daddy's closest friend and whose soft Scots burr and whimsical remarks delighted us, as they did his students. Dr. Lang loved to talk and sometimes, to our great amusement, would become so engrossed in his topic that he would forget his two o'clock class. On these occasions he would pull out his watch and cluck his tongue. "Too late now: They're only supposed to wait ten minutes!" Then he would give us his one-sided, mischievous smile and continue the discussion.

A few years afterward when Daddy died of a heart attack, we asked Dr. Lang to make the simple funeral remarks. Only the previous Tuesday Daddy had led the singing at the Rotary Club, and had never been in better form. Now it was again Tuesday morning, but this time his clubmates stood silently as Daddy's honorary pall bearers. When at noontime they all gathered at the hotel for the regular meeting, the spirit had gone out of the gathering. One by one the half-touched plates were pushed aside, and finally Dr. Lang was asked to read again his tribute to the absent member.

A friend told me later how everyone stood listening again to the gentle Scotch voice: ". . . His was a genial, generous, a friendly personality, and if today our thoughts are sad, it is because our pleasant thoughts of his friendly smile and gracious manner intensify our sense of loss. One of our poets has said that 'the best portion of a good man's life are his little, unremembered, nameless acts of kindness and of love . . .'" and so on to the end. It was a short speech for one who so much loved to talk but when Dr. Lang finished, there wasn't a dry eye in the room as with bowed heads everyone turned from the table. For the first time in many months there was no song.

Chapter Twelve

Uncle Hugo and the Crimson Tide

Ours was a football town. I recall one time when I was very small, Mother and her friends laughed over the name given to a new baby boy in the neighborhood. He was so large, everyone said, that his mother had named him Steven after "Big Steve," the star quarterback of what was then called the Thin Red Line. On Saturdays we would often watch the university football games from behind the windshields of our cars, parked in a row of others along the sideline fence. There was no stadium in those days, only a straggle of wooden bleachers with a handful of loyal spectators.

When, after years of drought, Alabama's team finally made the big time with an unbelievable win over top-ranked Pennsylvania, the town went wild. The celebration rivaled the one following the Armistice a few years earlier. Students snake-danced through the streets and literally painted the town. Long afterward when I was in high school, one could still see the faded legend: "Ala. 7—Penn. 0" on the side of the high railroad bridge on River Hill.

Daddy never missed a game, although I think it embarrassed him a little when Mother jumped up and down screaming herself hoarse, as she always did. To Daddy's bachelor brother Hugo, football was the very breath of life. Hugo was well-established in the cotton business at that time, making annual trips to New York and Europe to visit his buyers, but he never permitted mere buying or selling to interfere with any chore that he might perform for his beloved Crimson Tide. Hugo's official title was Graduate Manager of Athletics, but he had a hand in almost anything that needed doing—interviewing prospective players or coaches, scouting football rivals, arranging transportation to or from games—he always traveled with the team—supplying uniforms during the lean years and, at times, actually supporting impecunious players. There were few football scholarships then, and the rules were lenient. Hugo was generous to any worthy charity but, for a winning football player, the coach could count on Hugo for anything from a pair of shoes to a full scholarship.

When my friends and I were still small enough to walk to town barefoot, we invariably went first to Uncle Hugo's office on Broad Street, since he never failed to give us nickels or dimes. With these clutched in hand, we would later visit the drugstore with its high marble soda fountain for a cherry ice, which the man made by squirting red syrup over crushed ice in a paper cone.

Behind the plate glass window of Uncle Hugo's office stood the big rectangular tables which were always piled high with fluffy cotton samples. Occasionally, a sunburned farmer would be standing there while one of the men in the office graded his cotton by "thumbing" the bolls to judge the length of the fibers.

We could usually find Uncle Hugo at his big desk behind the cotton tables, leaning back in his swivel chair listening to a tall young player or one of the coaches, or some businessman who had dropped by to talk football. Hugo's office was a very crowded place just before a big game, because Uncle Hugo was always given a block of free tickets which he doled out to a long list of friends and relatives. One thing he rarely gave out, however, was a tip on the outcome of a game, because he abhorred gambling. It was the game itself that he loved, not the money to be made from it.

Uncle Hugo enjoyed football practice almost as much as the big game and seldom missed a session, even in rough weather. One winter, however, he contracted pleurisy and nearly died. I shall never forget how frightened I was when Grandmother Linka, with finger to lip, led me quietly into Hugo's darkened upstairs bedroom. I saw him lying there on the high carved bed like a stone knight on a cathedral tomb. Not that Uncle Hugo looked like a knight. His nose was much too large for good looks, and his hair was growing thin on top, but I had always seen him neatly, even jauntily dressed, a monogrammed handkerchief in his coat pocket, a fresh rosebud in his buttonhole, and a kind smile for a child or a pretty girl. At that moment, I had the horrible thought that perhaps he was already dead, but Hugo weakly turned his head, raising a skeleton-like hand to beckon me closer. I couldn't understand his hoarse whisper, but Grandmother correctly interpreted his gesture toward his trousers hanging limply on the wooden clothes stand.

"He says there's something special for you in his pocket," Grandmother said, smiling as she drew out a folded five dollar bill. Never having had such a large sum before, I could hardly think what to say.

Although he was invariably kind and courteous, it was always difficult to talk to Uncle Hugo. He had no fund of funny stories like my father, and I didn't know the language of the sports world Uncle Hugo loved. As frequently as our family saw him during his long life, I never felt that any of us except perhaps Daddy and Grandmother really knew him. There was always a sort of aloofness surrounding him like an invisible wall. I think now that he was a lonely man, despite the multitude of his friends.

On that occasion, after Grandmother led me downstairs, she

suddenly shed her sickroom manner and, much to my surprise, pulled me into the big front parlor and pointed toward the piano. In a rare display of temper, her lips set angrily in her small face, she told me, "Will you please look at what someone sent me this morning!" I looked at the piano, puzzled. All I saw was a tall vase of white lilies, which filled the room with their too-sweet fragrance.

"It's like a *funeral* spray:" she sputtered. "They think he's going to die, but I won't *let* him: And I know just what I'm going to do with these." Grandmother swiftly pulled the dripping lilies from the vase, flung open the back door, and hurled the offending flowers into the shrubbery. Then, wiping her wet hands on her apron, she smiled at me with a hint of mischief. "I feel better already. You just wait and see: I'll have him up and around again in no time at all!"

Despite Grandmother's devoted nursing, however, the doctor shook his head over Uncle Hugo's weakened condition. It was true that he was on the mend, the doctor said, but Hugo must be reconciled to a long stay in his bedroom during that treacherous weather. But the doctor might as well have talked to the wind for all the attention Hugo paid when he learned from a visiting coach that Spring training was about to begin. The first day of practice found Hugo in his usual front row seat in the bleachers, looking thinner, but as eager as a boy just out of school.

If Uncle Hugo had any other illness from that time up to his extreme old age, he never let us know about it. Indeed, he made it a constant practice to keep his body in first-rate condition. Not only did he never drink or smoke, but he offered my brother and me five hundred dollars each if we would refrain from drinking or smoking until our twenty-first birthdays. He bought an elaborate exercising bicycle contraption to use during the times when he couldn't go hunting or fishing and helped develop several fishing lakes in the area, from which he supplied his friends' tables with trout and bream.

Nearly every year, too, he invited the reigning coach and a select group of fishing buddies to accompany him on an elaborate expedition to the Everglades, usually around Boca Raton, where Hugo had made friends with a boat captain and his pet alligator named Joe, who followed the boat through the bayous, rising to the surface on call to receive his handouts of fish scraps. I have many snapshots of Uncle Hugo proudly surveying his enormous catches, but most of the fish were given away to his friends for, as in football, he loved the sport for the pleasure it gave him.

There was one story that always brought chuckles from Uncle Hugo's friends because his teetotal habits were so well known. He never tried to inflict his own ideas on those who thought otherwise and frequently his fishing pals took along their favorite libation. Hugo and a group of friends made one such trip to a large lake in the southern part of the state and an old Negro was hired to row the boat. It seems that party had included a quart of bourbon and, during some injudicious moving around, the small boat capsized, plunging all the merry crew into the deepest part of the lake. As each one emerged choking and gasping, they discovered that Uncle Hugo was the hero of the day, for clutched tightly in his hand as he rose to the surface was the bottle of whiskey!

Apart from sports Uncle Hugo's chief avocation was pretty girls. Sometimes he was jokingly referred to as "Dean of Women" at the university, but he was never seen with one college girl. He enjoyed a group of four or five. Perhaps it was because he was aware of his own limitations as a conversationalist that he liked to hear the girls' chatter and laughter. Occasionally, Hugo would take his girls to a movie or for a spin in his beautifully kept Cadillac. More frequently he would honor the girls with a ride to Birmingham for dinner and a show.

I was invited on one of those jaunts when I reached college age, and a friend who had been on several of the trips told me that the routine never changed. I could believe her. It was an axiom downtown that people set their watches according to Uncle Hugo, who always went up the post office steps at exactly seven forty-five and put his key in the office door at five to eight. In Birmingham, we went to the Tutwiler Hotel for dinner, where Uncle Hugo invariably recommended the meringue glacé. Loving sweets himself, he always offered them to people he liked. There was sometimes a whispered debate among the more sophisticated girls as to whether they dared to smoke after dinner. Uncle Hugo never said anything, but the girls somehow sensed his feeling that smoking was unladylike. Afterward the party would adjourn to the Bama Theater, and, after a movie, he drove the girls at a leisurely pace for the sixty homeward miles, often stopping on the way at Bessemer for ice cream. It was said that Uncle Hugo was the only man that Dean Agnes Ellen Harris, who was notorious as being something of a tyrant, ever permitted to take her coeds out of town on an unchaperoned trip.

Dean Harris had become an admirer of Uncle Hugo when she had consulted with him about his scholarship girls. Each year he offered six loan scholarships to girls who had shown unusual character and ability in high school. An impartial committee of business friends handled the details, but Uncle Hugo liked to make the personal acquaintance of these girls and offered them small kindnesses which they remembered gratefully in later years. I know several of his old "girls" corresponded with him for years. I suspect that Uncle Hugo actually derived more pleasure out of the Birmingham trips than his girls, however, as he grew older, and as the changing college life began to offer more exciting entertainment than dinner in a slightly staid hotel.

My family and, indeed, the whole town and campus held Uncle

Hugo in such respect and admiration that it was hard for me to imagine what he must have been like as a child. When I asked Daddy about it, he told me that Hugo had always been a good boy, but that he did have one annoying habit. He would jump out of bed at the crack of dawn and would then go knocking on doors to wake up everybody else in the house. Their father vowed that his youngest son would grow up to be the best businessman in the family, a prediction which later came true, although my grandfather did not live to witness it.

Often when Uncle Hugo was on a business trip, Grandmother would ask me to stay with her. I loved to follow her around the big, quiet rooms as she did her chores and to sleep with her at night in her great Lincoln bed with its towering headboard carved with columns and scrollwork. Sometimes when I went with her into Uncle Hugo's bedroom, perhaps to dust or to put away his clean clothes, I would look musingly at the miscellany of pictures and pennants and think that this room was, in a way, a record of his life.

On the whole, the room had a strongly masculine flavor. An interior decorator would have shuddered at the ugly but comfortable Morris chair, the realistically painted porcelain lion's head, the white Parian hunting dog being attacked by wolves, the faded college pennants and souvenirs on the walls and the massive walnut wardrobe. Once I explored that wardrobe, fascinated to find above the assorted guns and hunting garb and row of well-cut suits, two fine leather boxes containing a collapsible silk top hat and a real English beaver.

Although I had rarely known Uncle Hugo to read anything except newspapers and magazines, the rows of well-filled sectional bookcases attested that once he must have been a devoted reader of popular romantic novels. This discovery confirmed my belief that at heart Uncle Hugo was a sentimentalist in a world growing increasingly pragmatic. The most incongruous item in the room was a small brown teddy bear propped on an open shelf, reminding me that once long ago this had been the playroom of a lonely little boy.

Grandmother was an orderly soul and occasionally she fussed about the clutter in Uncle Hugo's room. "One of these days," she would murmur, "I'm going to take down some of this junk and put it out in the storeroom where it belongs." She would glare with particular disdain at the lifelike portrait of a Victorian beauty with one lush bosom prominently and to Grandmother's modest nature, horrifyingly displayed. "And why he wants that thing I'll never know!" she would exclaim, flinging her words back over her shoulder at another bright chroma of a bustled beauty daintily lifting her ruffled skirts to display a well-turned leg as she negotiated a mud puddle. I would smile to myself, knowing that Grandmother would never dare to make such comments in Uncle Hugo's presence. Actually, like any well-trained German housewife, she consulted Hugo's wishes before making even the smallest decision or change, whether it concerned food, the house, or the garden.

It was no wonder that despite Uncle Hugo's generosity he did become rather self-centered. Though he squired a long succession of pretty widows, causing much speculation in town, the family never took the rumors seriously. Looking back on the women I had known who attracted Hugo, I can see now that they all had certain qualities in common. They were warm, pleasant, down-to-earth women, with an easy naturalness about them that was far removed from Grandmother's shy modesty. But not one of them would ever have been truly at home behind those haughty white columns. Perhaps the girls were his avenue of escape, like the alluring beauties on the walls of his bedroom, from the comfortable but changeless routine that must have grown at times a little boring.

Old friends who knew Hugo as a gay young man-about-town,

in the days when he plucked his mandolin to the "coon" songs and sugary ballads then in vogue, said that he had once been deeply in love with Annalee Fitts and she with him, but her devoutly religious mother had discouraged the romance. Probably no one knew the true story except the ones most involved, but I well remember lovely Miss Annalee, who always seemed, even when she was middle-aged, like the real life heroine of one of the old romances Hugo had loved to read. Often people wondered why she never married, and why, even during the flapper styles of the twenties, she stubbornly clung to her high, wavy pompadours, the starched and ruffled shirtwaists, and sweeping floor-length skirts of her youth. Perhaps it was Annalee's own quiet rebellion against a domineering mother who was rumored to have a "heart attack" whenever anyone opposed her.

Grandmother often laughed at the fact that Hugo's one desire when he traveled was to return home as quickly as possible. In New York, he cared for nothing except a visit to Yankee Stadium or an occasional musical comedy. Europe was merely a place to market his cotton and to purchase occasional gifts for his friends and relatives. Only once had the even tenor of his life been interrupted for more than a short time, and it took the international cataclysm of World War I to do that. He was past draft age, but feeling that, as a bachelor, he should contribute his share, Hugo volunteered for duty with the American Red Cross.

He served on the important but little publicized Italian front, his mission being to supply food to the isolated outposts guarding the Alpine passes against the Germans. He remained overseas for many months after the Armistice, helping in the hospitals and with the rehabilitation of the men who had been half-starved in German prison camps. A battered trunk which I delighted in exploring told the story of those days in the Alps: a long, narrow picture-map with a jagged line of mountain peaks marked with crosses and dotted trails; heavy socks, sweaters, and hooded, fleece-lined jackets; boxes of medals and odd souvenirs carved from shell casings by former prisoners and given in gratitude to their benefactor; dozens of snapshots with backgrounds of small tents against snowy mountains; and, in the place of honor in its velvet jewel box, his greatest treasure, the Italian Cross, awarded to him at Santa Caterina, Val Furva, where he had been director of the rest camp "Generale Pershing."

In flowery, halting English, with typical Italian emotionalism, the citation reads in part, ". . . this modest and excellent officer . . . indefatigible in the development of his duty, enthusiastic and passioned with Alpine life, with sound good judgement for the necessities of our troops, he had brought, everywhere . . . precious contributions to the moral elevation of our soldiers. But his work has not stopped at this development . . . He wanted to bring, in person, to the troops in the very first line, even to the most advanced outposts and to the lone sentinel in front of the enemy, the comfort of the word and of the help of the great American fatherland. To Capanna Milane, to Garvia, to Forna Glacier, to Tresero's peak, to Camosie Pass, on the great heights of König-Spits, anywhere necessity manifested the work . . . was carried out. Through difficulties of every kind, often obstructed by the nearness of the enemy, to which he answered not caring, with serene and youthful daring, following tenaciously and resolutely to the accomplishment of his duty . . ."

Uncle Hugo's answers to my questions were characteristically concise. "What was the scaredest you ever got?" I wanted to know as I sat turning the pages of his photograph albums.

"Well," Hugo drawled thoughtfully, his gray eyes glancing past me as if they saw again those endless white mountains, "there was a sort of little basket on a cable. One of the fellows had managed to climb up the other side of the mountain to anchor it, though they were shooting at him all the way. Then another one of our crew climbed into the basket with the supplies to be pulled across. It went okay until he got about to the middle of the chasm. Then something happened—I don't know what. Maybe the load was lopsided or maybe it was a gust of wind, but whatever it was, the basket flipped over, and out he went! We just stood there and watched him fall—thousands of feet down to the bottom. Then the basket came back for me, and *I* had to climb into it." I trembled, feeling suddenly cold in the warm, familiar room.

"Why was it so important to get the food over right away?" I persisted "Couldn't you have waited to be sure it wouldn't happen again?"

"As things turned out," he answered, "it was a good thing we managed to get across. You see, there was this one company of men that was holed up in a cave guarding the Brenner Pass. That was the main way the Germans had to get down into Italy and they'd managed to get a ring of sharpshooters all around the place so that nobody could get food to those poor fellows. When we finally reached them, they were almost starved and almost ready to give up. But they were a mighty brave bunch of men!" He cleared his throat and paused in retrospective admiration, "Do you know what they were getting ready to do? They had that place all fixed and ready to blow themselves up and the pass, too. We arrived there with the food just in time!"

Many years afterward, in a letter filed with his will, Uncle Hugo left his trunk full of war mementos to the local chapter of the American Red Cross. In the same letter there was another bequest which saddened us all with its unconscious pathos. "It is my wish that my Italian war medal be given to the son of my niece Peggy who bears my name."

Besides the war, the only other major disruption of Uncle Hugo's life was Grandmother Linka's death from a cerebral hemhorrhage. She died peacefully in her sleep after years of increasing weakness during which Uncle Hugo surrounded her with loving attention and the best nurses. Those who did not know him well wondered whether Hugo would now give up the big house, which Grandmother had willed to him, and perhaps move to an apartment or hotel. However, the family was not surprised when Hugo not only would not consider giving up the house but adamantly refused to change a single thing in it from the way Grandmother had left the place. I can remember her wickerbasket of crochet patterns sitting on the library table for nearly a year until I finally requested it as a keepsake.

We had a big laugh over an incident some months later which well illustrated Hugo's stubborn intractibility. The town had acquired a block of land for a badly needed new hotel—all of a city block, that is, except one corner lot containing an ancient, rather dilapidated clapboard house out of which the lone occupant steadfastly refused to move.

"That old fellow must be crazy," Uncle Hugo declared. "Why, they've offered him a fortune for that beat up old house." The same hotel committee, in an effort to buy Uncle Hugo's house a year earlier, had not only offered Hugo an enormous sum of money but also a free suite in the new hotel for life. Uncle Hugo had, of course, turned down this offer without a second thought—and would never have seen the parallel between himself and that "crazy old fellow".

Hugo gave free rent in his empty house to a succession of young great-nephews and cousins who came to attend the university. Finally he made a permanent arrangement with his bachelor friend Charlie Golson, whose pleasant companionship gave consolation to him and to all of us during Hugo's declining years.

There were many times during the sometimes turbulent family life of our growing-up days when we felt a pang of pity for Uncle

Hugo along with our affection and growing admiration for his position in the community. After Grandmother's death, Mother fell into the habit of inviting Hugo over for Sunday brunch, for which she would prepare feather-light waffles or small hot biscuits and platters of scrambled eggs and country sausage, or occasionally his favorite oyster omelette. I think he looked forward to those mornings when he became for a little while part of a family, and he always arrived with a big box of Whitman's chocolates.

I think, too, that the breakfasts helped to bridge the gap between Mother and Uncle Hugo, for I felt that Hugo had never really approved of his brother's marriage. Mother was the epitome of everything Hugo found faintly disturbing in modern women—bridge games and cocktail parties, their outlandish dances, their informal clothes and manners, and, above all, their independence. Uncle Hugo's world, in turn, represented for Mother all the stifling restrictions which she opposed with all of her strength.

If we chanced to see my uncle's dignified figure climbing our front steps at any hour past sundown, however, Mother's typical reaction was to call out, "Oh, Lord, here comes Hugo!" Then somebody would be directed to "Run, hide my drink and pour me a glass of ice water!"

Later, when, aging and alone, Mother and Hugo were the last members of the family left in Tuscaloosa—with Daddy and Grandmother dead and the grown children scattered across the map—the two drew together in mutual dependence, although I believe that even then, they never really adored each other's company.

While Daddy's fortune had vanished during the financial crash that preceded the Depression, Uncle Hugo, predictably, had invested in utility stocks and government bonds. Not only did his fortune increase, but honors earned in his long years of public service began to shower upon him. Newspapers throughout the state ran the story of Hugo's purchase of a fine antebellum mansion to save it from destruction which he presented to the city as the Friedman Library in honor of his immigrant father, "Because," Uncle Hugo said, "the people of Tuscaloosa were exceedingly good to all of those whom I hold dear, and they have continued to make my life—all down the years—an existence that could not have been bettered."

We were proud of our relationship to Hugo when he was presented successively with one award after another; the Algernon Sidney Sullivan Award in recognition of his aid to young people, an honorary degree of Doctor of Humanities from his beloved university, engraved plaques and tributes from the Chamber of Commerce and the Rotary Club which he had helped to found, and his name—Victor Hugo Friedman Hall—above the door of the new specially equipped dormitory for athletes at the university.

The honor that pleased Hugo the most was a complete surprise. One night a group of high school boys called on him with a special invitation and a guest ticket to attend their annual Spring band concert. To make sure he attended, the boys begged to have the honor of escorting him personally on the following Friday night. Mystified but pleased, Uncle Hugo accepted. On the appointed night, he was quite overwhelmed when he was led to the center of the stage to find that the entire concert, comprised of favorite old-time tunes and football songs, had been planned as a tribute to him.

Uncle Hugo's last illness began so gradually that for months we could not convince ourselves that there was anything really wrong. He forgot things, but then elderly people do. His once immaculate clothes now were often wrinkled and his figure stooped a little, but his routine was still unvarying.

Sometimes he complained that he had no work at the office because, as he said, "The government has taken over the cotton business." This, too, we had been hearing for some time, and we paid little attention.

Accordingly, it came as a real shock when Uncle Hugo's youngest partner told us that he had finally persuaded Hugo to sell his cotton business. "I don't know whether you've noticed it, since you don't see him every day like we do, but his mind is failing. He's got so much money he can't even count it, yet he imagines he's going bankrupt. This is the first year we've ever lost a penny in the business, and it's scared him half to death. That's the only way I'd ever have persuaded him to sell. Believe me, the way things are going, we were lucky to get this good offer!"

The new owners had purchased his firm's name, too, a name Hugo had made very well known throughout the region. His big chair was still in its old place behind the cotton tables, and things did not seem very different, except that now Hugo had nothing to do but talk football with his friends. This was the one thing that never changed.

Our worst trial was his driving. After several narrow escapes when he let the car wander off the pavement, he was persuaded to give up the trips to Birmingham with his girls. Several of Uncle Hugo's friends began to refuse to ride with him, and people were amused when the rumor circulated that while in the company of one of his pretty widows, Uncle Hugo had been arrested for driving too slowly! The townspeople grew accustomed to giving Hugo's big car a wide berth as he drove slowly and serenely down the exact middle of the street, looking neither to right nor to left.

His worried nieces, Louie and Adele, with whom he customarily spent Christmas in Dothan, finally summoned the courage to tell him that they would flatly refuse to let him visit them again unless he would hire someone to drive him down. Hugo promised faithfully and hired his yardman on the spot. When the appointed day arrived, Uncle Hugo was right on schedule, calmly steering his brand new Lincoln Continental up the driveway. When he stopped, the back door of the car flew open and there appeared before the girls' startled eyes the shaking Negro, "so frightened he was almost white," Louie told us later.

"Law, Miss Louie," the yardman moaned, "I tried my bes', but he wouldn' lemme even staht to drive! 'Naw suh,' he sez, 'I hired you for the trip, and I'll *pay* you, but I'm doin' the drivin'.' But, Miss Louie, ain' no amount of money gonna git me back in dat car agin!"

It was only natural that when the following summer Uncle Hugo had a slight stroke and was carried protesting to the hospital, our first impulse was to beg the doctor to order Hugo not to drive until he was well. "You needn't worry about that," said young Dr. Moody, old Max's son, shaking his head sadly. "His driving days are over. I expect he's had several of these small strokes, and he'll probably continue to have them. Each one will do a little more damage. It's the beginning of the end."

When Uncle Hugo left the hospital, we made him as cornfortable as we could in the big, drafty house. He wouldn't, of course, even consider a nursing home, and we were all accustomed to letting him have his way. We moved a small bed downstairs to a sunny corner of the drawing room and hired a cook and a pleasant trio of nurses. Once he grew accustomed to the new routine, I think Uncle Hugo really enjoyed all the attention he was getting. It had been a long time since he had been petted and fussed over, and capable Mrs. Morris won his heart by taking him out to ride on good afternoons.

The other nieces and I took turns staying with Hugo until everything was well-organized; the house had been so long neglected that we had our work cut out for us. It was a symptom of Hugo's illness that he had ceased to notice his surroundings: the cracked plaster, the stopped-up plumbing, the yellowing of beautiful old linens, the tarnished silver. We took turns at veritable orgies of housecleaning which infuriated poor Uncle Hugo who wanted everything to be left alone and in its original place. When we had finished our operations, he would sometimes totter on his failing legs into the big front parlors to make sure each vase or picture remained in its exact place.

One day I arrived to find Adele and Louie in a fit of hysterics, both of them black with grime from cleaning the long-closed china cabinets. Adele had a towel wrapped around her head. "I was afraid the bat would get into my hair," she explained.

"A bat!" I squealed, momentarily forgetting Uncle Hugo, but the two quickly silenced me as they led me out of his earshot to tell their story. The bat had flown out of the long-closed pantry and, although they were frightened half out of their wits, they had bravely chased it through the house with brooms and mops to no avail. When Louie's son Mike, who was attending the university, had come to the front door, the two women rushed out to greet him as their savior.

"At last, a man!" Louie cried, handing him the broom. "Thank goodness you're here. We've got to keep that thing away from Uncle Hugo." Mike soon proved a frail reed. The two sisters again burst into laughter as they recalled how Mike had ducked under the table the first time the creature had circled the room.

"I'm sorry," he said, gulping, "but I just don't like bats."

It was Charlie Golson who saved the day in his easygoing, matter-of-fact way. "We get them every now and then," he admitted apologetically, "but it won't hurt you." Whereupon he calmly shooed the bat upstairs and into the bathroom where it drowned unceremoniously in the toilet.

After those first weeks, we left matters in the hands of the capable nurses, and for more than a year the household ran smoothly. There was a constant stream of visitors and gifts but, as time passed, Uncle Hugo's mind gradually grew vaguer. We were never sure how much he understood. Finally, even football seemed to lose its interest for him, though he would perk up a little during a visit from Bear Bryant, coach of the now mighty Crimson Tide which had been proclaimed number one by no less a person than President Kennedy himself in a public ceremony.

We never dreamed that there was destined to be one last football game for Uncle Hugo, and it came about in an unexpected way. Mrs. Morris, the head nurse, would occasionally ask her husband to sit with her patient so that she could have a few free hours to do errands. This was quite agreeable with us, as Mr. Morris was a kindly fellow whom Uncle Hugo liked at once. It happened that Mr. Morris was a great football fan and that this was the afternoon of the biggest game of the season. The town was jammed with excited people, and the tickets had been sold out for months.

As Uncle Hugo sat dozing in his rocking chair, Mr. Morris turned on the radio, and the familiar tones of the football announcer filled the room. The reaction was electric. Uncle Hugo rose from his chair like an old firehorse smelling smoke. "Bring me my coat," he demanded. "We're going to be late for the game!" Now Mr. Morris was a simple man who did not know quite what to do in this unfamiliar predicament, and he did exactly as he was told. Most people did with Uncle Hugo—he had that air about him—and then, of course, Mr. Morris loved football, too.

The two drove out toward Denny Stadium, around which cars were parked for more than a mile in every direction. "Just drive right up to the main gate," Uncle Hugo directed. "I can't walk very far." Again Mr. Morris did as he was told, driving the big car right over the curb and up to the gate, as nearly everyone else was now inside the stadium. It was not until he had helped Uncle Hugo out of the car and up to the turnstile that Mr. Morris realized that neither of the two had tickets as Uncle Hugo had given them all away.

If Mr. Morris was dismayed by this, Uncle Hugo was not. "We're going to the press box," Hugo told the startled gatekeeper as he pushed past him, holding to Mr. Morris's sturdy arm. "They know me up there." Up to the press box they went. I would like to have seen the expressions on the faces of those present as Uncle Hugo calmly seated himself among the pressmen as if this were an everyday occurrence.

Unfortunately, his burst of energy did not last long. Even football could not hold his attention any longer, and Hugo was soon nodding in his chair. Finally Mr. Morris whispered that perhaps he'd be more comfortable in the car. Forced to agree, Uncle Hugo consented to be led back down to the Lincoln, which by then was completely hemmed in on every side. As the distant cheers rose from the great stadium where the Crimson Tide triumphed once again over the rival, Uncle Hugo slept peacefully through his last football game. He died not long afterward, a few months past his eighty-sixth birthday.

Until the day after Uncle Hugo's death, the family knew no more than our fellow townsmen what he intended to do with his house as none of us ever dared to ask. We knew that in his will our grandfather had intended that the house remain in the family, but Uncle Hugo knew that none of us could afford to keep up the place. Various pressure groups had been after the property for years—the Y.M.C.A., a new courthouse, the new hotel, the giant Sears, Roebuck, and Co. store—and it was rumored that Hugo had turned down enormous sums of money. Privately, we were sure that he'd donate the house to the university or to the town, and we were right, though the order was reversed. According to his will, the house was to be offered first to the city and, if it refused to accept the gift on Hugo's terms—the preservation of the house as a meeting place for clubs and civic groups—the same offer would then be made to the university.

We were sitting around the dining table in Uncle Hugo's house when the will was read. As we were all travel-weary and exhausted from the ordeal of the big funeral and the multitude of guests, my brother-in-law had mixed drinks for one or two who felt in need of restoration. The lawyer raised his eyebrows in amusement as he read aloud: "Item five. No sale of alcoholic beverages shall ever be allowed in the present Friedman home, nor shall any function be allowed therein where alcoholic beverages are served." It was Hugo's voice speaking from the grave!

Poor Uncle Hugo, I thought, feeling faintly irreverent and disloyal. He wanted very much to preserve things exactly as they were.

Most of the bequests in the will and most of the stocks in his bank vault were what we expected. Everyone was remembered— each leading Christian and Jewish congregation in the community, a Negro charity, the Scouts, his outstanding girl students, and his athletes. Since we had been compelled to take over the management of his affairs during the long illness, there were few surprises. There was one strange item in the vault, however, so strange that even now, years later, I often think about it. It was a letter addressed to Uncle Hugo and postmarked from a town in the northern part of the state. It was tied around and around with knotted string and Uncle Hugo had written across the front of the envelope in heavy black handwriting the firm notice: "This letter is to be destroyed unopened in the event of my death."

We did as Uncle Hugo wished, of course, as we usually did, and the letter was left for the bankers to destroy. Could there have been somewhere in the past life of that gentle man a secret love or a secret guilt? I will always wonder.

There were no tears at Uncle Hugo's death because his real self had been dead for a long time. In the newspapers there were long write-ups concerning him and a special television show telling the story of his life and illustrating it with pictures culled from the old albums. But the tribute I think Uncle Hugo would have liked best if he could have known of it came from his own Crimson Tide. In the middle of football practice for the big game, Coach Bear Bryant blew his whistle for silence.

"I have just learned of the death of Hugo Friedman," the coach told the assembled players. "I would like us to pause for a moment of silent prayer for this man who has done so much for our team throughout the years."

Chapter Thirteen

Dream House
for a Dollar a Day

During the Depression it was Mother who convinced Daddy that they could have fun in summer without making expensive trips. His wooded acres must be full of beautiful picnic spots. Brought up in an inland town without even a creek in which to swim, Mother had always been fascinated by the Black Warrior River. Although we had customarily gone to the North Carolina mountains or the Florida gulf coast for vacations, there had been one memorable summer years earlier when, with several other families, we had actually camped for two weeks in tents on some of Daddy's land near Lock Fifteen. Now that there was no longer enough money to travel, Mother reminded Daddy of that beautiful spot, hoping to persuade him to build a small cabin there.

We drove out the narrow, winding road on the following Sunday and found the gray cliffs and tall pines as picturesque as we had remembered them, but Daddy pointed out that during the twenty-mile ride we had passed only one or two wagons. "There are some rough customers in these hills, Laurie. They say up here that if you see a freshly painted house, the man's bound to be a moonshiner. If we had a cabin here, there'd be times you and the children would be alone. It just might not be safe!" Mother was compelled to agree, but she did not abandon the idea of a cabin and, almost in spite of himself, Daddy began to grow interested.

There were fewer cars and no paved roads outside town in those days, but people enjoyed pleasure riding. It was Daddy's invariable custom to take us for a drive on pleasant Sunday afternoons. One day he recalled a swimming hole and "baptizing creek" to which his father had taken him as a boy. He thought there was an abandoned early settlers' shack nearby, if it had not collapsed. After what seemed an endless ride through the rockbound hills—actually the drive was only fourteen mies—we found the sandy, weed-grown track leading through the pine woods to a weathered, swaybacked cabin with two rooms and a leanto kitchen.

At first Mother was doubtful. However, there was a mud—and-stick chimney and a clear, bubbling spring close to the cabin. After walking down the steep hill to investigate the swimming hole with its miniature waterfall, Mother pronounced herself satisfied. This was also an isolated spot. but since Daddy owned several hundred surrounding acres, he knew many of the hill folk and pronounced them all to be honest church-going people. From then on, that little cabin—which my teenage friends appropriately nicknamed "Tore-Down"—witnessed many enjoyable weekend gatherings. Mother had the walls of one room ripped away and replaced by a screened porch which was also enlarged to surround the kitchen. We only needed a filled ice-box, folding cots, and our victrola to complete our furnishings.

"Tore-Down" was our second home for several years, but the cabin had one big drawback which loomed larger as time went by. Each time we went to swim, the homeward climb up the hill seemed to become steeper, and Mother would often sigh, "Oh, if only I could build a little cabin right beside the pool . . . I think I'd name it 'Toe-hold,' because that's all I'd need, just a toe-hold on the creek bank." One day she saw her chance to make the dream come true.

"Dogwood Lodge"—we talked Mother out of "Toe-hold"—came into being as a result of two misfortunes not unusual during the Depression. Daddy had loaned money to a "jack-leg" sawmill operator near our cabin who, finding himself in difficulties, had absconded with the cash on hand, leaving Daddy with the worn out sawmill machinery and a few thousand feet of unfinished oak boards. "Why couldn't we use that lumber to build a log cabin on the creek?" Mother tentatively asked.

"Now, Laurie, you know we haven't any money," Daddy protested. "The woods are full of pine logs, but that's not the problem. Workmen have to be paid in cash."

There the matter might have rested had not the other fortuitous circumstance occurred. Old Mr. Herring, one of the hill farmers from whom we occasionally purchased milk and eggs, came with a long face to the cabin porch one weekend. His two sons, having lost their jobs in the city, had come home with their families and were camping in his yard. Did we by chance have some odd jobs they could do? They'd work for a dollar a day and be glad to get it.

Mother seized her opportunity. "Sam, I've saved forty dollars from the housekeeping money. That would last twenty days. Let me have that oak flooring, and at least we can make a start . . ."

Daddy never had a chance when Mother got that certain look in her eye. The very next day, outlining the future rooms in the dirt with a stick, Mother showed the Herring boys where she wanted the cabin to be. For months Mother had been collecting magazine pictures of balconied hunting lodges, high-roofed ski retreats, and mountain chalets. She knew exactly how the cabin should look. Now, at last, she could realize her dream.

As it happened, Daddy became unexpectedly busy at the office during those weeks and was not around to restrain her. When he at last found the time to journey out to view her efforts, he could only stand in open-mouthed amazement. "Ye gods, Laurie!" he exploded. "Do you realize you've made this living room forty by thirty feet! I don't see how a wall of logs that size can be braced and supported, and how in the world will you heat it? It gets cold in these hills, remember?" Mother, however, was undismayed and, as usual, her enthusiasm was contagious. Daddy was a civil engineer, after all, and the problem of stresses and support provided an interesting challenge. Indeed, it was Daddy who contributed the crowning glory of Dogwood Lodge—a rock chimney so *enormous* that it would probably endure for centuries.

The soaring log walls and huge fireplace of Dogwood Lodge soon became the show place of the countryside. The men who had worked on the house would often bring their families to gaze in wonder at the cathedral-like arches of the living room with its log steps and balcony and massive sliding doors. Daddy had discovered an unlettered country carpenter who, on the rare occasions when he was sober, proved to be a genius at converting hand-planed cedar logs into furniture. The great round dining table built around a large cedar stump was his masterpiece. Members of our family, their relatives and friends have gathered around that table each summer for more than forty years, as Mother and Daddy moved to Dogwood Lodge early in May and stayed until the frosty nights of late October sent them regretfully back to town.

Daddy loved the lodge. It was he who contributed the rock dam for a larger swimming pool and cleared the woodland trails. Hopefully, he supervised planting the gardens and an orchard by Ed and Evie Bouyer, the Negro couple he had persuaded to move into "Tore-Down." Yet Dogwood Lodge was really Mother's possession—Daddy even had it legally recorded in her name—and we rarely thought of the lodge apart from her. All during the winter, she drove out to the lodge on sunny days with her gardening tools to set out bulbs or flowers, to transplant wild hydrangeas and rhodendrons, or to supervise the ever impatient Ed in his construction of a rock wall or a new kitchen cabinet.

Indeed, Dogwood Lodge was never finished. I sometimes wonder if that was not its attraction for Mother's restless nature. After the four of us were married and began to bring our own growing families for their annual visits, Mother always had some new project for us. She would corral us into refinishing the floors or sanding an old cabinet from Grandfather's office or building a rock terrace, as each year the lodge would sprout a new room or porch.

Dogwood Lodge became an ideal place for the informal entertaining Mother had always favored. The Up-to-date Club had its Spring meeting there when the dogwood and redbud were in bloom, and sometimes Mother would spend the day strolling in the woods with Theresa Strode. When Mother was in the hospital during her last illness, a letter from Theresa recalled those walks and the two women's discovery of a lovely spot they called the "Blue Grotto" as among the happiest experiences of her life.

On several occasions the entire Longshore family—forty or fifty strong—would congregate for a reunion, and I am sure that in everyone's mind, Dogwood Lodge and Mother became forever linked in their memories. There were some dances and drinking parties when the lodge was first completed but, aware that Daddy's straitened purse would not permit the freeloaders of former years, Mother devised a practical scheme to keep expenses within bounds. Her friends were simply requested to bring their own liquor and at larger gatherings, everyone chipped in for the supper pot. Mother's favorite dish was spaghetti, for which she had devised a rich meat sauce cooked separately in a big cast iron pot.

I remember one occasion during the second World War when, having planned a supper for several hundred guests to make money for Bundles for Britain, Mother blithely spent the whole day on the golf course. To stop the persistent worried questions about preparations for the evening, she replied with a shrug, "Really, there's not a thing to do except start the sauce and put flowers on the table."

I think the reason this party, like her others, was so successful was that she allowed her guests to do as they pleased. They strolled in the woods or along the creek, ate where they liked, or harmonized around the big log fire, and, of course, as always, thoroughly enjoyed themselves. Mother's entertainments were really "happenings," long before the term was invented. In later years, countless visitors recalled those days at Dogwood Lodge as unforgettable experiences in a uniquely beautiful setting.

Chapter Fourteen

New York
on Fifteen Dollars a Week

To Mother, New York was a mecca of excitement and glamor. Before the Depression put an end to such extravagance, she and her friends made frequent pilgrimages to the fall openings of the new plays. For weeks beforehand, they would have scanned the reviews in the *New Yorker* and the theater pages of the *New York Times*. Then, armed with choice tickets, they would descend upon the city for a round of shows and shopping and visits to old acquaintances. For me, New York had a different attraction. It was the center of the world of books, and, with naive confidence in what I had been led to believe was a budding literary talent, I dreamed of becoming a part of that world.

My chance came on my twenty-first birthday when Uncle Hugo, true to his promise, gave me five hundred dollars upon my faithful assurance that neither liquor nor cigarettes had touched my lips. Employment opportunities were practically nonexistent in the South of those days, so it was not too difficult for me to get my reluctant parents' consent to start my great adventure. When I arrived in New York in the summer of 1932, the Depression was just beginning to show its real power over the city. However,

I came provided with traveler's checks, my master's degree, some glowing letters of introduction, and a vast ignorance of city life. But I was not afraid, then or later.

From the moment I left Grand Central Station, with my wardrobe trunk lashed firmly to the back of a taxi, I fell captive to the spell of New York. Each day in a kind of trance I wandered from my temporary haven in a girls' hotel, mesmerized by the towering immensity of the buildings, the unfamiliar sights, odors, and sounds peculiar to the waterfronts, the Bowery, Chinatown, Harlem, and the garment district. Having always been surrounded by the slow drift of life in a Southern small town, I was fascinated most of all that here was not one city, but dozens of them—each tightly circled and distinctive, busily living out its life within its selfmade boundaries. I yearned to explore all those communities firsthand and savor their strangeness.

Dismissing taxis as being too expensive, I walked for hours in the invigorating New York air without growing tired. I took a childlike pleasure in zooming through the mazes of subway tunnels that miraculously connected teeming Times Square with the far-flung campus of Columbia University in a mere twenty minutes. Best of all I loved riding on the upper deck of a Fifth Avenue bus on a sunlit day, from which vantage point I could observe the poised and modishly dressed women shoppers who made me feel awkward and ill-dressed when I passed them on the street. I visited museums and art galleries, strolled through the parks, and rode up the elevators of the tallest buildings to look out over the city.

Every night I went to the theater and that was a vintage year: Helen Hayes in "Mary Queen of Scots," Katherine Cornell in "Alien Corn," a revival of "Showboat" with Paul Robeson, "Porgy and Bess," and dozens of lesser attractions half forgotten. Mealtimes, too, were voyages of exploration. I soon learned that my familiar Southern foods—those small hot biscuits and chicken fried in bread crumbs—seemed unknown, and I followed the restaurant guide in the *New Yorker* and got acquainted with the special dishes of each country. I sampled Italian dishes on Bleecker Street, Swedish smorgasbord, eggs *mornay* at the Brevoort sidewalk café, black mushrooms and sour cream at a little place run, I was told, by real Russian aristocrats who had been banished during the Revolution. Some of those dishes I liked and some not, but I gamely tried them all.

It was a glorious two weeks stopped only by my realization that, at that rate, my money wouldn't last very long. Somehow I had to spend a year in this city which meant that I must stop dabbling. It was time to take the plunge into job hunting. Pulling out my letters of introduction, I mapped my campaign strategy. Thus began my awakening.

Three or four of my letters were adressed to slightly older former recipients of Uncle Hugo's scholarships, who had been working in the city for some time. Two of the girls invited me to dinner in their little apartments and shook their heads sadly at my lack of training—no shorthand, no marketable skill in typing. I pinned some hope on the third girl, who was within actual touching distance of the world of literature. She was a reader for one of the big publishing houses and gave me a letter to her boss. This gentleman received me courteously but sadly. He was laying off half his staff that very week; my new friend was lucky to be staying.

"Moreover, my dear girl," he said. "if you want to write, go home where your roots are. Becoming a reader is like running your mind through a sewer tank. You become so saturated with other people's ideas that you never get around to expressing your own." Later, I often thought of this advice, but with each rejection, I became more stubbornly determined to stay.

My next letter was addressed to Amy Loveman, co-editor with Henry Seidel Canby of the *Saturday Review of Literature*.

She was a long-time family friend who had often visited her aunt in Tuscaloosa and, although she was not blood kin, I had always called her Cousin Amy. The magazine, which long ago as a young woman she had helped to found, was barely able to support its staff, she told me, adding that that very morning she had bought an unneeded article from a young writer simply to enable him to buy milk for his baby.

Although Cousin Amy couldn't help me find work, she welcomed me to her apartment on upper Riverside Drive, where I was instantly charmed by her father, then ninety-six years old and one of the most delightful characters I'd ever met. Those spacious, old-fashioned rooms became my second home, especially on Sundays. I believe now, looking back, that the close bond that grew up between her and me came about partly because, through my overflowing enthusiasm and sometimes humorous tribulations, she vicariously relived her own youthful days.

Father Loveman and I also became great friends and I never ceased to marvel at his unflagging zest for life. Although he already knew several languages, he was then learning Spanish, he told me, to keep his mind active. His love for poetry delighted me, especially when he thundered out in his rich voice some stirring stanzas from Kipling, whom he called "a real man's poet." Father Loveman did not dwell on the past, although he did lament the modern ignorance of quality. He had his shoes, for example, made especially by hand so that they would really fit. And on one occasion, he took a sentimental journey which I would have loved to have witnessed.

Cousin Amy came home from work one day and was frightened out of her wits to find her father missing from his accustomed leather chair by the window. A phone call to her brother's Wall Street brokerage office helped her piece together what had happened, and Father himself strolled into the apartment a short time later to supply the details.

Amy's wealthy brother, having been invited out of town for the day, had placed his limousine and chauffeur at his father's disposal on the chance that the old man might enjoy a ride. Father did indeed: He told the startled chauffeur that he thought he'd just ride over to Princeton, New Jersey, to see his alma mater which he hadn't visited in about seventy-five years. Once there, he went directly to the President's office where he was welcomed by surprised officials who showed him proudly around their beautiful modern buildings, but Father Loveman felt lost and disappointed. There was, of course, little he could recognize, as he might have expected. Surely there was some place, he thought, that hadn't changed. Suddenly an idea occurred to him, and again he and the chauffeur drove off—this time to Shakerstown, Pennsylvania, where he had a leisurely afternoon in the peaceful village that prided itself on clinging to the past!

Cousin Amy gave me sympathetic encouragement, and, whenever I dropped by her office, I caught brief glimpses of such prominent literary figures as Christopher Morley and William Rose Benet. However, those visits were not getting me any closer to a job. I had been postponing delivering my last letter because it held my greatest hope. Carl Carmer was then assistant editor of *Theater Arts Monthly*. I was certain he'd assist me if he could. Carl, as hearty and red-faced as I remembered him, hugged me warmly but informed me regretfully that he was on the verge of losing his own job, and his magazine folded not two weeks after I arrived. With it folded my last hope of a literary career.

At that point, I might have grown discouraged if Carl and Betty Carmer hadn't taken me in—literally. For the next two weeks, their living room couch served as my bed. The tiny spare room of their Greenwich Village apartment was already occupied by a young writer—Inge somebody, they called him—who was toiling over his first novel. I could hear his erratic typing as we discussed my problems in the cluttered living room, Carl pacing the floor with loud, cheerful talk and expansive gestures. Betty, whom I had not met before, looked suntanned and exotic, with sharp features and dark eyes, her straight hair pulled back into an unfashionable knot, and her long fingers clasped around her bright-colored full skirt. She did not look motherly in the least, but I soon discovered that Betty had a penchant for people down on their luck.

Jobs could still be found, she told me, although maybe not exactly what I had in mind. She herself had taken a boring clerical job that paid enough to keep the two of them going, although she admitted she and Carl had just sold their car, which they did not really need. They had just located a perfect job for Isobel as a church secretary. Then, of course, they had to tell me Isobel's story because she was coming for supper.

Every day, Betty began, as she climbed the stairs past the second floor apartment, she could hear a girl's heartbroken sobbing. Finally Betty had knocked on the door. Isobel had lost her husband, a young preacher, after less than a year of marriage and had come to New York from a small town in New Hampshire to be alone with her grief. She was thin as a rail, Betty continued, had not eaten properly in weeks, and her hands trembled so badly she couldn't hold a coffee cup. It wasn't enough simply to fatten her; she needed a whole change of scenery. Betty decided to take Isobel home to New Orleans with her on the pretense that she needed a "companion" for the trip. The combination of Southern sun and New Orleans cooking had done wonders, as I soon saw for myself when Isobel arrived, a blue ribbon tied around the shoulder-length brown curls framing her face. She looked more like seventeen than twenty-seven.

Carl Carmer himself, according to hometown gossip, had been on a hard luck road before Betty found him, unshaven and drowning his sorrows in a French Quarter restaurant near the place where she was working with a Little Theater group. He had left the university under a cloud—he just could not resist pretty girls, everyone said, and it appeared there were some who couldn't resist him either. My family didn't pay too much attention to the stories, and I had always liked Carl, enjoying the electric atmosphere he created.

At least he was never dull! In fact, I have heard many of Carl's former English students say that he was one teacher they could never forget.

Sometimes I think he was like an overgrown small boy who mischievously took special enjoyment in puncturing our Southern complacency and conservatism. This has now become a national sport, but it was a new experience then. Some of my fellow townsmen have still not forgiven him for tacking the names of prominent local citizens onto some of the less savory characters of his famous book, *Stars Fell on Alabama*.

From the beginning, Betty knew exactly how to handle Carl and I suppose that is why their childless marriage has held together for all these years. On one of those first Greenwich Village evenings, while Betty was putting together her delicious tossed salad in a wooden bowl, Carl began rather pompously to propound his theory that married couples should date other people occasionally so their life together wouldn't grow stale. Betty didn't say much, but a few evenings later Carl came home to find a curt message that Betty was "out to dinner." His huffing and puffing reminded me of Shelley's father-in-law who advocated "companionate marriage" for everyone but his own daughter!

Although the Carmers insisted I was no trouble, I couldn't continue to occupy their only couch indefinitely and I began to search in earnest for a place to live. Carl solved that problem, too, after inquiring among his friends, and that is how I met Mrs. Mc-

Cue. For thirty-five dollars a month I became the occupant of her best front parlor in the old brownstone at 11 Bank Street. The room had a real fireplace and enormous windows. All I needed to buy to feel at home was a bookcase, a bed, an electric grill to go behind the screen, a bundle of small logs, and a bouquet of half-wilted roses for a quarter from the vendor at the nearby subway entrance. Sandwich makings and milk could be purchased at the delicatessen across the street, and I soon discovered that at the gleaming white orange bar on the corner, I could buy real orange juice, coffee, toast and marmalade for a dime.

Mrs. McCue was the first native-born Irishwoman I had ever met, and her thick brogue delighted me. She was a plump, florid woman with a wide, humorous mouth and straight, yellowish-gray hair that was always falling over her spectacles. The only phone in the house was in her basement apartment and often, between bouts of job-hunting, I'd stop there for a friendly talk. Her favorite topics of conversation were her house—which was her great pride—her childhood days in Ireland, and her cat, Tom, in that order.

Her father had been a flax farmer in Ireland, she told me, a solid man who owned his land and was not beholden to anybody. When he died, however, the family had to sell the farm and there wasn't much left beyond what would keep her mother. When Wanamakers had advertised for Irish girls who knew how to make lace, offering them free passage to America, Mrs. McCue had signed up for the trip, although she was barely fifteen. She had been one of Wanamakers' best lace makers for five years and might have been there yet, she said, except for an accident.

One winter day as she was hurrying to work, Mrs. McCue had slipped on the icy pavement and broken her wrist so she could never make lace again and, as she hadn't learned to read or write, she didn't know what was to become of her. "And thin wan day," she ended dramatically, "as I was walkin' along the street, I shut my eyes and asked God what to do, and whin I opened 'em, there was this very house standin' empty like the answer to a prayer." She had put up her insurance money as a down payment and had been here ever since.

Tom was a very large cat, with a bitten ear and numerous scars attesting his virility, who lived in the back yard which was overgrown with weeds and brambles, Mrs. McCue wouldn't have anything cut because "this way it's like a little bit av Ireland right here in New York." That Tom, now, she said proudly, had learned to unhook the back door and even to turn the doorknob, and she just had to give him the run of the house. In fact, the roomers had dropped into the habit of borrowing Tom for a day or two whenever they had mice and perhaps *I* might be needing him one of these days! She was right. I soon took my turn for Tom's favors.

It was from Mrs. McCue that I first heard of Hugh Troy, her most famous boarder. Hugh was a well known prankster in those days. In fact, one of his escapades had been recounted in the *New Yorker*. It had occurred while Hugh was a tenant of the very room in which I was living. The story concerned the time Hugh bought a park bench and placed it beside an identical bench in Central Park. After Hugh and a fellow prankster had enjoyed a leisurely afternoon sitting on their bench, they calmly got up in plain view of a flabbergasted policeman, and began to lug the heavy bench down the walkway.

"Say, where are you going with that bench?"

"But, officer, it's *our* bench!"

"Yeah? Well, you can just tell that to the judge."

"We will!"

And of course, they did! Hailed into court, Hugh, to the surprise of the judge and the delight of the audience, with a dramatic flourish pulled out his bill of sale for one park bench!

Mrs. McCue enjoyed all the Hugh Troy stories except the one

of which she had been the victim. "Do you know what they say he did naow, in his foine Park Avenue apartmint? He's painted himself a ring of cockroaches around the bathtub, to 'make him feel at home', he sez, 'since he's moved uptown from the village!'" She was indignant at this aspersion cast on her spotless bathrooms, both of which she scrubbed twice a day. Still, the bathrooms were old-fashioned and drafty, with cracked linoleum and yellowed walls.

I shared the bath on the second floor with a harassed-looking young couple whom I occasionally saw hurrying along the hall, always with tousled hair and wearing bathrobes. One day my kind-hearted landlady let slip the fact that she hadn't charged the two any rent for several months. In all that time they had not found any work except as occasional clerks, and Mrs. McCue was worrying about whether the couple had enough to eat. Lately, they'd been selling their clothes and furniture, she reported, and the only good thing they still owned was a red leather armchair that had been a present from the workers he used to boss. I never met this couple, as they soon moved away, but my heart gave a sickening lurch that afternoon when I came home from job hunting and saw a fine red leather armchair outside the door awaiting its new purchaser. It was the same day I got my first job.

I became a waitress in the Florentine Room of the Schraft restaurant on Fifty-seventh Street. The closest I would come to greatness would be to serve morning coffee to the habitues of nearby Carnegie Hall. Though the salary was ten dollars a week plus tips, it was a job, and when my daily stint was finished, around two o'clock, I could eat my fill of delicious food. Moreover, there was still time to hunt for a better job in the afternoons. My living expenses came to exactly fifteen dollars a week so, if I watched every penny and never touched my traveler's checks except for room rent, I just might manage to remain for a year in this fabulous city.

Actually I stayed a year and a half. As in any love affair, the events of those first few months in New York remain clear and untarnished—the first meeting of new friends, the first job. The weeks that followed, however, seem like the rapidly changing patterns of a kaleidoscope. After a few months as a waitress, I became a salesclerk in B. Altman's department store, where the munificent salary of eighteen dollars for the six-day week was balm for sore feet and the end-of-the-day collapse from sheer exhaustion. I decided I had earned the right to be extravagant with that extra three dollars and gave myself a real treat on Sundays.

By that time I was growing a little homesick for the sight of trees and green fields, I had fallen into the habit of spending Sunday afternoons rambling through Central Park—after standing enraptured before my beloved Rodins and Rembrandts in the Metropolitan Museum. Now I was beginning to feel a little hemmed in by the overpowering Manhattan skyline. Where could I go for three dollars and find lots of big trees, I asked an amused elderly clerk in the bus terminal. He suggested Middle Neck, on Long Island. The bus ticket would cost me thirty-five cents, and he was right about the trees. I was even more excited to discover a riding academy with miles of beautiful bridle paths where I could ride for only two dollars an hour.

The riding academy was around the bend in the road from Eddie Cantor's beautiful estate. Some half-hope had prompted me to pack my boots and riding habit before leaving the South, and on my next trip to Long Island I began the first of many enjoyable horseback rides through that lovely area. Occasionally, on blustery days, some friendly young people I had met would smuggle me into a nearby country club, but I had too much pride to trespass often where I couldn't afford to be a member. I was quite satisfied to enjoy the trees and the horses and then return refreshed to my job at the costume jewelry counter.

I even turned down a chance to go to the Army-Navy football game to keep that stupid job—and then, right in the middle of a dull February—I was fired! Tough luck, the store's personnel manager said, but sales were slow . . . and so they were, not only there but everywhere. Daily I made the rounds of more than fifty employment agencies. There didn't seem to be *any* jobs. Finally, in desperation, I agreed to sell dresses at Russek's department store on straight commission. As I was in the "cheaper dresses" department, where all the dresses were fifteen dollars, my commission would be three dollars on each sale. The first week I earned nine dollars, the second week six. At that rate I was getting nowhere fast. Then, at the lowest ebb of my fortunes, I encountered an old acquaintance from the South, Charlcie Hedge, another of Uncle Hugo's scholarship girls.

Through her, I got the most memorable job of my brief career. The New York stage had been hit hard by the Depression. Unemployed actors and would-be actors were walking the streets, many too proud to ask for assistance. At that point, a concerned group of wealthy people calling themselves The Citizens Committee in Aid of Stage Relief hit on the idea of a huge benefit performance at the Metropolitan Opera House on a Sunday evening in March. They set up shop in an empty office and prepared to plaster the city with posters and to inviegle established performers into contributing their talents for the cause.

Charlcie, who had met some of these wealthy women during a former job as a secretary at Republican National Headquarters, had been hired to run the office, so she, in turn, hired me as her assistant. Mainly, I was an errand girl, but I wouldn't have missed those errands for the world, for in delivering the appeal letters, I came face to face with such people as Ed Wynn, Jimmy Durante, Irving Berlin, Fannie Brice, Fred Astaire, Clare Luce, and the incomparable Ethel Barrymore. One time I had to go backstage while a performance was in progress and was permitted to watch from the wings. That show was great fun, even though I had trudged a mile through a winter rain to get there, and though I was still being paid only fifteen dollars a week.

Charlcie and I knew, of course, that in April we would both be out of work again. Meanwhile, we were always amused by our inside view of the millionaires at work. I remember one occasion when a telegram from a mysterious Olga, delivered to the wrong office, brought an embarrassed blush to one of our plutocrats who had apparently being playing hanky-panky. Another time, we were startled to find that our "bosses" refused to honor a reservation for a block of tickets for the wife of the owner of one of New York's largest department stores because her "credit was no good!" I must admit, however, that those wealthy people, like the performers, gave freely of their time and money. They were truly concerned, and the benefit was a tremendous success.

My memories of that job were perhaps a little more fragrant than I might have expected. One of the "come-on" gimmicks for the benefit was the sale during the performance of hundreds of bottles of donated perfume which was supposed actually to have been made from the same formula as Chanel No. 5. Charlcie and I were presented with more than a dozen leftover bottles as an extra "thank you" for our efforts. When I went home from New York a year later, one of those bottles leaked its potent contents into my wardrobe trunk and the odor was so strong that I had to store the trunk in the attic. More than ten years later, I could still sniff that Chanel No. 5 whenever I opened the attic door.

I had many small jobs during that year, although no other quite as exciting as the benefit. One job that I rather enjoyed was running the express elevator at 60 Wall Tower on Wall Street. I had been hired because the elevator starter was from Mobile, Alabama, and it reminded him of home when he heard my accent. I liked three things about that job: the uniform was becoming and it was furnished free, which saved me money on clothing; although we were not allowed to sit down in the elevators, there was a comfortable parlor where we could take a fifteen minute "break" every two hours; and, finally, I loved the view from the top! I never got tired of looking out of those magnificent skyscrapers.

Of course, many of my New York experiences were unglamorous. I soon lost my earlier naiveté, though never, thank goodness, my sense of adventure! I met dozens of people and was disappointed in only a few; I learned to keep my mouth shut about the South because New Yorkers prefer to believe their own myths. I voted for "Little Flower" La Guardia and marched in the giant youth parade to promote his reform movement. I fell in and out of love—but that's another story.

There were times when I was lonely and I think there's nothing quite like the loneliness of a big city where one is surrounded, almost oppressed, by masses of uncaring people. Then, to remind me vividly of my own first days, there were the visits of my two friends from home.

June came first. She was the daughter of Champ Pickens, founder and promoter of Alabama's famed Blue-Gray Football Game, and she arrived, exactly as I had, armed with high ambitions and glowing letters of introduction but alas, with no traveler's checks. Her funds would last two or three weeks, she said, if she could share my room. June's Irish-blue eyes and witty conversation soon charmed Mrs. McCue, but her ambition was quite another matter. Having recently acquired a law degree *magna cum laude*, June aspired to clean up Tammany Hall, no less!

Cora Carr Brisky arrived unannounced a few days later, armed with a master's degree in bacteriology but with no more money than June. Cora Carr, too, had planned to share my room, and June and I were both delighted, as Cora Carr was great fun. She was a tall, breezy girl from Colorado whose dynamic personality and venturesome spirit had made her a campus favorite. Her New York goal was high, too, although not as unrealistic as June's. Cora Carr planned to work at Columbia's new Medical Center or another of the great medical foundations and would accept nothing else. Cora Carr's tall tales from the West and June's wisecracks soon made my parlor a sort of salon for displaced Southerners. The Village was full of them in those days.

At night, we slept sideways in my big bed with our feet in the three chairs. Inevitably, and all too soon, the girls' money ran out. Just before the end each of them, without telling the other, applied at Schraft's for a job as waitress—and both were turned down. Their departure from New York took some of the sparkle from my great adventure. For the first time, I began seriously to think about my own future, although for a while longer I was still held by the fascination of the city.

During my last job as a file clerk for a freight company— again at my apparently top wage of eighteen dollars a week—I put the extra three dollars to use by taking night classes in social work at New York University. I suppose the plight of the poor people trapped in the slums was beginning to stir my conscience and, in my youthful idealism, I wanted to do something about it, although I didn't yet know what. Never before having gone to school with Negroes, I was impressed by the earnestness and dedication of the young colored students and the knowledgeable realism with which they tackled the seemingly insoluble housing problems of Harlem.

I thought about the miserable conditions back home in the South of the Depression and began to wonder whether I, too, could help do something about them. Before this half-formed desire had a chance to cool, I sent off an application to the Child Welfare Department of Alabama. I did not know whether to be sorry or glad when the department accepted the application, and I realized that I was not to spend my second Christmas in New York after all.

There were still so many things to do, so many places to explore. I had just discovered the Staten Island ferry made familiar by Edna St. Vincent Millay's poem, and the trip miraculously cost only a nickel. I hadn't yet taken the boat trip around Manhattan Island, and much as I loved the tall buildings, I had never been to the top of the Empire State Building. That cost a dollar while others almost as tall were free! I knew I must see those wonderful Goyas in the Spanish Museum. I had gone only once and now would never see them again. I think I knew somehow, even then, that I would never come back to New York. I think I felt in a subconscious way, too, that there was something good about leaving while the magic still existed. As I taxied to the station, an early morning snow had carpeted the streets. I'll never again see it turn to dirty slush, I thought.

Chapter Fifteen

Mary Bacon

Most of Mother's friends did not become real people to me until I was grown up. I knew which ones played golf or bridge, and which couples came to the evening parties, but those I knew and liked best were in the small group which often had lunch together: Nell Clarkson, Jean Moody and her cousins Sarah and Ira Moody, who were sisters-in-law, and Mary Bacon Clabaugh. Mary Bacon, with her deep, rich voice and sparkling wit, always fascinated me. A room came alive when she entered it and, like Ethel Barrymore, she was always center stage, with tall, regal bearing, flashing dark eyes under the crown of smooth black hair, and animated conversation.

It was the sinking of the "Mary Francis" that brought Mary Bacon alive to me as a tragic figure. Mr. Sam Alston, a wealthy banker in our Pinehurst neighborhood who loved children, had made it a habit to give free boat rides once a year to the children of Tuscaloosa. My brother and I begged for the treat and, as we were too small to go alone, it was decided that Mammy would take us to Riverview Park on the streetcar. It was a hot, dusty day, and we found the park jammed with excited children. After a long wait, our turn finally came for the short ride upriver. It was not until the homebound streetcar deposited us on our Pinehurst corner that we knew anything had gone amiss.

We were met by a frantic crowd of neighbors searching for their children. Cousin Eva Persons was hysterical and kept screaming at us, "Where's Clarence? Haven't any of you seen him? My God! I thought he was with you!" Only then did we learn that on the ride after ours, the overloaded boat had sunk while making too sharp a turn. Twenty-seven children and four adults had drowned, among them Mary Bacon's son, Sam Clabaugh. Mary Bacon had a baby girl named Mary and would later have three more daughters, but she never became reconciled to the loss of her adored little boy. It was the first time death had come close to someone I knew, and it made a deep impression.

For weeks people talked of the tragedy, of the all-night search parties, the acts of heroism, of Mr. Alston's agony and of Ben, the boat's pilot, who went insane from grief. A brave twelve-year-old girl had saved the life of little Sam Clabaugh's uncle, Congressman W. B. Oliver, and the elderly man had tried to hold onto the boy but the child had slipped away from him. Mother's friends told of how Mary Bacon had shut herself in her room, refusing to see anyone or even to care for her baby girl.

Some years later, the two older Clabaugh girls, Mary and Betty, became friends of my sister Virginia, who was six years younger than I, and they often came to our house to spend the day. Even as a small girl Mary, as dark and vivid as her mother, showed the precocious intelligence and imagination that would later make her one of the nation's most highly honored professors. She was always the leader in the children's games. I also remember one period during which Mary made a rule that everything the children said must be spoken in rhyme, and her facility amazed me. Like her mother, she was never at a loss for words.

Although no one opposed Mary's leadership, Betty was more

popular. With her blue eyes and light brown curls she already showed traces of the charm that would later serve her well as the wife of a diplomat in the State Department in Washington. When the third daughter, Jean, with her round face and straight brown hair, became a student at the University of Alabama, she once told me that Mary was the smart one and Betty the pretty one, but she was just plain old Jean. But Jean, too, had her share of the family charm. She was a happy person whose four lovely children would bring much consolation to Mary Bacon in her later years, as Jean's son Clay bore a marked resemblance to the little brother who drowned.

I never knew Doris, the last daughter, although she became a friend of my youngest sister, Peggy, but in snapshots of her I could see a distinct likeness to her mother. Of the four sisters, she was perhaps the one closest to her mother in wit and spirit. There was a reflection of Mary Bacon in the humorous comments scattered through Doris's *Virgin Islands Cookbook*, written at her home on the island of St. John, where her talented Russian husband was manager of the large United States National Park.

When the Clabaughs moved to Birmingham, where Mary Bacon's husband Sam had been offered the vice-presidency of a major bank, their place in Mother's circle of friends was hard to fill.

Nearly every week there had been friendly battles over the bridge table, though there was a short time during the twenties when Mah Jong was the rage. During their last year in Tuscaloosa, they had reverted to duplicate bridge, a challenging game in which Mary Bacon's excellent memory made her a strong competitor. The move to Birmingham, however, did not end the friendship with my parents. Mary Bacon came back for frequent visits, which were always the signal for a round of the parties she loved. During the football season, the Clabaughs' big new house was the scene of many convivial gatherings of Crimson Tide supporters, and Mother and Daddy were often overnight guests in Birmingham.

When the news of the Clabaugh divorce came, it was almost as great a shock as if they still lived among us. Divorce, at that time, was something that did not often happen to people we knew. I was too young to participate in the heated discussion of pros and cons, but I soon found that there were more cons than pros, for in spite of her gift for enduring friendship, Mary Bacon's barbed wit often had a sting. Then, too, there are always envious understudies eager to pull down a star performer. People still talked of a country club dance during which someone had sneaked into the ladies' lounge and slashed Mary Bacon's new mink coat into ribbons—a mystery that was never solved.

I remember Sam Clabaugh as a courteous, quiet man, prematurely bald, who loved his children and was liked by everyone. Looking back with the hindsight of years, I can see that for someone of Mary Bacon's tempestuous temperament, life with him would probably have become inescapably boring. Things seem to have come to a head when Mary Bacon's wealthy bachelor uncle, Congressman W. B. Oliver, became head of the prestigious Ways and Means Committee and an increasing power in Congress. He suggested that Mary Bacon preside as hostess in his Washington establishment, a position which must have been a tempting plum to a woman of her proven social talents. "Birmingham's not big enough for her," said her enemies. "Now she wants to queen it over Washington."

As an added inducement, Mr. Oliver was said to have offered Sam an important and remunerative post in the capital. The trouble was that, for all his gentle manner, Sam was a stubborn man. Moreover, he had made an important place for himself in Birmingham and he loved his work. He had recently become president of a large life insurance company and was absorbed in plans for its new skyscraper building. Mary Bacon went to Washington without Sam.

Only Doris accompanied her mother, for the older girls were by that time away at college, Mary at Vassar and Betty at Randolph-Macon, while Jean, a less dedicated student, had chosen the University of Alabama. Mary Bacon must have gloried in her new freedom. We didn't see her during those years, but we pictured her capturing new admirers in glamorous Washington circles. Then we began to hear strange rumors. Mary Bacon was being squired around the city, it was reported, by a young admirer from Mobile, fifteen years her junior. Perhaps she was only flattered by his attentions, we thought. Then the bomb fell. They were actually married.

I simply couldn't understand it. I had known Billy slightly as one of the older and more sophisticated boys at the university and could see how he might be swept off his feet by a handsome older woman. Yet when this strangely matched couple made their first visit to our house, there was Mary Bacon, whom I had thought of as a rather worldly and perhaps slightly selfish woman, looking as radiant and love-stricken as a young girl in the flush of her first love affair. Billy came from a prominent, well-to-do family but he had no personal fortune. In fact, at that time he didn't even have a job. They had a romantic plan of going to live in the French Quarter of New Orleans, where they both hoped to find jobs while Doris attended Sophie Newcomb College of Tulane University.

Much to everyone's surprise, however, the unusual marriage seemed to be going smoothly. When the Alabama team played in the Sugar Bowl, Mother and Daddy visited them in their Pont Alba apartment across from the Cabildo in New Orleans' Jackson Square. Mother reported that Billy had quite a gift for collecting and refinishing antiques, that their small apartment was charming, and that Mary Bacon was still completely absorbed in her new husband. Of course, the doomsayers were eventually proved right, as they so often are, but the marriage lasted for seven years and might have lasted longer had it not been for World War II.

Soon after Pearl Harbor, Billy was drafted into service in the Pacific and out of Mary Bacon's life. During the long period of waiting, she became a house mother at Sophie Newcomb College, a congenial post where she made many new friends. We didn't often hear from her during these months, nor was there any word of Billy. Finally the rumor came, and was later proved true, that he had fallen victim to the charms of a young American girl in Hawaii and had asked for a divorce. Mary Bacon did not see him again.

About this same time, three other blows fell—disasters never seem to come singly. Doris began having frequent asthma attacks, and the doctor recommended that she be sent North to school, out of the humid New Orleans climate. Consequently, Mary Bacon was alone when the second blow came, the sudden marriage of her ill and aging uncle, Congressman Oliver, to his secretary, a much younger woman.

Mary Bacon was both shocked and angry, as were her two sisters, Jeanette and Willie. When the three girls were orphaned, they had been taken into their rich uncle's home in Eutaw, Alabama, and treated as adored daughters. They were educated at good schools—Mary Bacon at Agnes Scott—and had always been led to believe that they would be his heirs. "You needn't worry about the future," he had often told them. "I'll see that you are well taken care of."

When he died, however, not long after the marriage, the sisters found that his entire fortune had been left to his new bride, with an admonition to "take care of his nieces and see that they had everything they needed." Mary Bacon's vociferous outrage was soon vented freely in the parlors of her Tuscaloosa friends. She was never one to hold her tongue. "The very idea," she fumed, "of thinking I would go to this stranger and ask for money for my doctor or my dentist! I'd die before I'd ask her for a copper cent!"

The battle that followed furnished our town with conversation for months. Threatened with a court suit, the bereaved widow, who had taken up residence in the old home in Eutaw, was finally persuaded to settle a small income on the sisters, which was a sop to their pride but did not do much to assuage their hurt feelings. The whole dreary affair, on top of the breakup of her second marriage, left its mark on Mary Bacon.

Then came the third and most heartbreaking blow—the news that her daughter Mary, with her young husband Arthur Wright, had been captured in China and thrown into a Japanese prison camp. The younger Mary's love affair with China had begun early. She was such a precocious child that she had graduated from her Birmingham high school at the ripe age of twelve: As it seemed ridiculous to send her to college at such an age, it was decided that she would spend a year with her Aunt Willie and Uncle Ned Bell who were then stationed in China. They adored Mary and had no children of their own. Thus began Mary's fascination with China which later became the absorbing interest of her life.

After graduating from Vassar, she began the serious study of Chinese politics which would later lead her to fame. A *Newsweek* account of "The Wright Dynasty" states, "The Wrights met in Harvard's Chinese library while both were working on their Ph.D.'s. Later, they honeymooned in China so they could do further research and wound up spending two years in a Japanese prison camp." When hostilities began on the Chinese mainland, Mary and Arthur had been urged to leave with the other American nationals, but were so absorbed in their work that they couldn't bear to break it off. Both spoke fluent Chinese and had many Chinese friends, so they decided to convert their assets into gold and try to ride out the storm. Arthur's main field of interest was early Chinese and Buddhism, about which he would later write his book, *The*

Eightfold Path. Mary Wright had already begun collecting material on Chinese Communism for former President Hoover's museum at Stamford University of which she would become the curator. But that was all in the future.

During those endless months of imprisonment Mary Bacon had no real assurance that her daughter was alive, though she wrote long letters and never gave up hope.

Then arthritis struck—that most mysterious and baffling disease. Perhaps the months of worry and frustration helped bring it on. I will never forget the shock of my first sight of Mary Bacon after that final misfortune, though the awestruck faces and horrified whispers of Mother's friends should have prepared me.

"My dear, have you seen Mary Bacon? She looks awful, simply unbelieveable. I hardly knew her!" The gaiety of the homecoming party made it worse, somehow. She had always been the laughing center of such affairs. Now there she was in the doorway, a shrunken, witch-like creature, her once-straight back hunched into a curve, her expressive hands turned into talons. Only the eyes were unchanged, as bright and sparkling as ever, and the rich, vibrant voice was the same.

As soon as she began to talk, I could feel the wave of relief in the room as people began to respond to the familiar magnetism. "She's the same old Mary Bacon," I heard someone say. "She'll come out on top or die trying." Her humor was a little gentler, I noticed, and directed mostly at herself.

"It's a good thing I'm so poverty stricken that I can't try all these new miracle drugs," she said gaily. "Some of them have terrible side effects, so my rich friends tell me. I just stick to my aspirins and my packages of gelatin four times a day for protein, and it works like a charm!" It was impossible to remain ill at ease in the face of Mary Bacon's open acceptance of her own "rotten luck," as she called it, Later I heard her say with a chuckle to one of the men,

"Well, of course I'm being good! All the vices are so expensive."

I was reminded of a long-ago evening when I had watched the Dennis-Shawn dancers and of how the aging Ruth St. Dennis had created on the stage the illusion of a lovely young girl. Mary Bacon could create that kind of illusion. Many of her old friends who had been rather cool toward her since the divorce now felt a new sympathy for her misfortunes and an admiration for her courage. They outdid themselves in issuing invitations, and her visits to Tuscaloosa became more frequent. One summer, Mother drove her to Winston-Salem, North Carolina, for an unforgettable visit with Betty and her husband and babies, and a pleasant side trip to the Charleston Gardens. Then there was encouraging news from the Red Cross that Mary and Arthur were alive and receiving Care packages. Finally, at long last, the war was over and they were safely home.

Not only were they home safely, but they arrived in style in the private plane of General George Catlett Marshall, no less!

The event is described in an article about the Hoover Museum in *The Saturday Review*, and was later reprinted in *Reader's Digest*:

"Especially thrilling were the exploits of Arthur and Mary Wright, the latter now curator of the Library's comprehensive Chinese collection. The young couple were topping off their Oriental studies in Peiping when the Japanese clapped them into a prison camp. At war's end, when General George Marshall arrived in China to seek an entente between the Nationalists and the Chinese Reds, the Wrights, now collecting for the Library, wangled seats on his plane when it flew into Yenan, the Red headquarters. Here the Wrights obtained very rare records of the Chinese Communist movement. The Communists cooperated, even giving up the files of their official newspaper, all except a few issues which the impoverished editor had sold for wrapping paper. Mary recovered these by searching at the town market. When the Wrights returned home, they left contact men who continued collecting."

Mary Bacon gloried in Mary's and Arthur's achievements as professors at Stamford University and was especially happy over the birth of their two sons, Duncan and Jonathan. Arthur's father had at first rather resented the marriage of his only son to an unknown young woman, but he grew to love Mary and his grandsons. At his death, he left the Wrights more than a million dollars which was a cause of great rejoicing among Mary Bacon's friends, for the first thing Mary did with her new wealth was to establish a trust fund so that her crippled mother could live in comfort.

I have always regretted that I was not at home on the occasion of Mary's and Arthur's visit to Mother when they gave her a copy of Mary's monumental book, *The Last Stand of Chinese Conservatism*. My last recollection of young Mary is of the stubborn, mischievous little twelve-year-old I had taken to camp with her sister and mine one summer in North Carolina. I also regret that I was unable to get all the way through Mary's weighty volume Mother admitted that she, too, got stuck halfway through. But I came to know the grown-up Mary through her charming letters to her mother, which Mary Bacon often shared with us. Particularly fascinating were the letters describing the Wright family's round-the-world tour, for which they took a year's leave of absence, accompanied by a tutor for their sons. By that time, Mary and Arthur had moved from Stamford to Yale, where both taught Chinese history.

A *Newsweek* article of May 1964 said of Mary, "Last week still another distinction: Mary Wright was named a full professor in Yale's Faculty of Arts and Sciences, the first woman so honored. A tall, big-boned woman who walks briskly, Mrs. Wright specializes in Chinese politics. One Yale student says Mr. Wright's lectures have more polish and humor than those of Mary, who 'talks too fast for taking good notes.' But a fourth-year graduate student adds, 'They're both enormously stimulating. I couldn't do without either one.'"

When the Wrights bought a large, rambling fourteen-room house on Long Island Sound, where the boys could have their sailboats, Mary Bacon began going up for annual visits. She enjoyed the stimulating conversations with the Wrights' intellectual friends, and Mary wrote that all their friends were charmed with Mary Bacon. For her Tuscaloosa friends, however, there was one drawback. Probably influenced by her contacts in the East, Mary Bacon had become an avid Kennedy fan. "It would be all right," said Mother, "If she just wouldn't bring John Kennedy into every single conversation! You know people here just can't go for the Kennedys and it sort of gets their backs up. But that doesn't stop Mary Bacon!"

Meanwhile, Doris, the youngest daughter, had been having adventures almost as fascinating as Mary's. During the war her father, Sam Clabaugh, had been sent to England as a major in intelligence work. He was placed in charge of a project of smuggling talented refugees from behind the Iron Curtain and into the free world. Doris was among the group of young people who were chosen to assist him in this challenging and dangerous work. During this period Doris had a brief and unhappy marriage to a young man of the group, a marriage which was later annulled.

No sooner had Mary Bacon got over the shock of that experience than letters began to arrive from Doris filled with glowing descriptions of a young Russian opera singer with a glorious voice. It was easy to read between the lines that Doris' interest in Ivan Jadan was far more than merely patriotic. "Good Lord, Laurie," Mary Bacon mourned to Mother, "I'm afraid my daughter's in love with that Russian—and he can't even speak English!" This was in the Stalin era, when the Red Menace cast a big shadow over the world for most Americans. Mary Bacon's fears were soon confirmed. Doris and Ivan duly arrived in New York, and nothing would do but that Mary Bacon must come to the city to give her stamp of approval.

The penniless young couple found a refuge, as I had, in the hospitable home of our old friend Carl Carmer and his wife, Betty. The Carmers had recently bought a tall, three-storied Victorian house with spacious grounds overlooking the Hudson River above the city. As they were never able to resist helping talented people who were down on their luck, practical Betty had devised a clever plan. The struggling artists they assisted would be asked to pay for their bed and board by improving the house in some way. One artist even painted an elaborate and beautiful mural.

Mary Bacon, on her return from New York, laughingly described Ivan's contribution. "He loves to garden, so he's taken over the yard work, and while he's pushing the lawn mower he practices singing at the top of his voice—and his voice is simply beautiful. People passing by stop to listen and by the time he finishes the lawn he has quite an audience!"

Mary Bacon, like Carl and Betty, had fallen under the spell of the attractive and likeable Ivan and were all eager to help him make his way in America. Carl even managed to arrange a concert for him. The trouble was, he could sing only in Russian! I never met Ivan, but I have heard his glorious voice on a recording, so I, too, was saddened by their regretful conclusion that he would not be able to earn his living as a singer.

Eventually the Jadans settled in Jacksonville, Florida, where Doris had got a job as a teacher. Ivan, she wrote happily, was building them a house with his own hands, and she was expecting a baby. Relieved that her last daughter's troubles finally seemed over, Mary Bacon journeyed to Jacksonville to be on hand for the blessed event. Then the sad news came. The baby was stillborn, and Doris could have no more children.

But like her mother, Doris had the courage and resiliance to put the past behind her. I never learned how Ivan happened to meet Lawrance Rockefeller, who hired him to take over the planning and upkeep of his extensive gardens on the Virgin Island of St. John. But Ivan seemed to have the gift of making friends and of making things grow, gifts he has shared with thousands of people now that the one-time private gardens have become the United States Virgin Islands National Park.

Doris has become as much an expert on the history and ecology of her small world of St. John as her sister Mary on China. The charming *Virgin Islands Cook House Cook Book* written by Doris and Ivan was published by the *Sunday Magazine*, which went to newspapers all over America. It reveals an intensive study of the St. John herbs and other native products in such recipes as the one for Gobi Bread, baked in a calabash, with the final instruction, "Break this bread with friends who don't believe a calabash won't break if you bake in it!" Granny's Pone, to be eaten with ham, requires among other ingredients eight cups of grated local white sweet potatoes, four cups grated local pumpkin, and a cup of Tortola raw sugar.

Doris was also teaching the mostly black children of St. John to love and take pride in their rich heritage. She sent my sister Peggy a copy of her delightful "1974 Ivan Evironman Calendar of Virgin Islands Cultural and Natural History," with proceeds of the sale to go for environmental education. Each page is illustrated with the schoolchildren's own drawings, and the comments scattered throughout the calendar reflect the children's concerns as well as the historical events and ecology of the islands: "On St. Patrick's Day, Patrick catches a group of groupers"; "Ivan says, 'Let's keep a garden at Reef Bay for everyone to see all the old-time bush medicines growing." "Easter Monday—Ivan and Christine use safe natural colors to dye Easter eggs—beet juice, yellow prickle, onion skin and semper ivy," and also there are many references to herbal medicine lore, such as, "Granny roasts a piece of careta (century plant) to heal a sore on Erasmus' back."

Mary Bacon was finally able to see Doris' enchanting island for herself through Mary's thoughtful Christmas gift of a trip to St. John for her mother. I still treasure the Christmas card Mary Bacon sent me that year, a picture of her and Doris on their beach patio, with Mary Bacon looking radiantly happy and almost as young as her daughter.

Mary Bacon seemed determined not to let her arthritis interfere with her zest for new experiences. The trip to St. John had been so successful that the following year she planned a longer venture. "I've discovered," she told Mother, "that in England you can hire a wheelchair in the British Museum and even someone to push you around, so I don't see why I couldn't manage just as well as anyone." So off she went to England.

After further crippling attacks of arthritis, however, Mary Bacon could no longer drive a car and retained only limited use of her hands. Characteristically, she adjusted her living arrangements in a way that would give her both independence and companionship. Her sister Willie and Ned Bell, who had retired, had built an attractive home on the shore of Mobile Bay, where they were later joined by the widowed Jeanette and her young daughter Suzanne. Mary Bacon had a small but well-planned apartment built onto Willie's home. "Everything in it," she said, "is planned so that I can manage easily—stove, windows, everything!" She spread out her poor, maimed hands expressively. "Of course, when I get sick of my own cooking, I can go over to Willie's for a real meal and Ned is a superb cook!"

It was a beautiful setting, the green lawn with its giant live oak trees draped in Spanish moss stretching down to the blue water of the bay. Next door was the large home of Carl Carmer's first wife Doris and her engineer husband, and in the nearby town of

Daphne was the quaint little Episcopal church where the son of an old Montgomery friend was the pastor. A steady stream of friends arrived for visits, while Jean and her attractive brood were a short drive away down the coast at Pensacola.

Sometimes there was the stirring excitement of a "jubilee," when millions of fish were mysteriously impelled to swim landward to throw themselves gasping on the beaches. Mary Bacon loved to talk of these rare events which created excited gatherings of natives from miles around, with the attendant campfires, fish fries, and general rejoicing. One time she cut short a visit to Mother because there were rumors of a possible jubilee and she didn't want to miss it.

Mother frequently drove to the coast to visit Mary Bacon and her sisters. I imagine she particularly enjoyed the late afternoons, when it was the invariable custom to spend the "happy hour" with tall glass in hand, watching the spreading sunset from the shelter of the great trees. When Mother returned from these visits, she often spoke wistfully of perhaps buying a bit of land on the bay and building a small cabin, but we all knew the mood would pass and that her own Dogwood Lodge would win out in the end.

Mary Bacon lived far into her eighties, outlasting Mother by ten years, and for the most part those last years were peaceful ones. After Mother's death, I kept up with Mary Bacon through Ira Moody, whose lovely retirement home in Destin, Florida, was near our own second home there. We always looked forward to visiting with Ira and to the good talk about our old Tuscaloosa friends as we sipped our drinks and watched the sunset over the bay from her hospitable porch.

One day she had sad news for us; a heartbroken letter from Mary Bacon telling of Mary Wright's death from lung cancer. Arthur had written the details of their last evening together. They had sat on the balcony and reminisced about all the wonderful times they had shared. Mary had smoked a cigarette with him. There had been no pain. She died that night in her sleep.

Inevitably, the time came when Mary Bacon could no longer manage to dress herself and keep house. She and her sisters visited the Sisters of Mercy Nursing Home a short distance down the bay shore, and Mary Bacon wrote Ira a long letter describing it. "It's a beautiful, quiet place with trees and flowers and a big, glassed-in sun porch overlooking the bay," she wrote. "I think I'll be comfortable there." Then, on a wistful note, she hoped there would be congenial people to talk to. "Some of the faces are so empty,"

I hope she did find friends in the two years she had left before her death at eighty-six. But I don't like to picture her among those empty faces. To me she seemed ageless—a venturesome, restless person, vibrant with husky laughter and sparkling talk. I think of Walter Savage Landor's epitaph, "I warmed both hands before the fire of life. It sinks, and I am ready to depart."

Chapter Fifteen

Mama Sayre, Scott Fitzgerald's Mother-in-Law

When we moved to Montgomery, where my husband had obtained a position as a state accountant, Marjorie Noble soon became one of my closest friends. We had met as volunteer swimming instructors for a summer day camp which our small daughters attended and, on discovering that we had many mutual interests, we'd drifted into a habit of lunching together afterwards while the children played. We had been surprised to discover that our mothers had been classmates at Judson College and that Marjorie's mother had even spent a school holiday at the Longshore home in Columbiana. Marjorie also shared my love of books and writing; she had written some quite good poetry. Perhaps this talent, in addition to her delightful wit and zest for life, was the reason Zelda Sayre Fitzgerald, her mother's sister, seemed to feel an especial warmth toward "Noonie," as the Sayre family called Marjorie.

When Marjorie learned that my mother had been acquainted with Zelda and Scott during their long-ago visit to Tuscaloosa, she told me stories of Zelda's girlhood as the spoiled and adored baby of her family. Sometimes Zelda would have to babysit for her small niece, a chore which she detested as it restricted her own activities. Once she placed the frightened little girl in a tree too high for her to descend alone, and admonishing her to "stay right there till I get back," she and her friends went off on their roller skates, returning an hour later with a candy stick and a warning, "Don't you *dare* tell on me!" Another time she pushed Marjorie down a steep hill in a small wagon which the child had no way to steer or to stop. Somehow, people always forgave Zelda such thoughtless escapades because life vibrated with excitement when she was around.

When Marjorie was herself a teenager she had visited Zelda and Scott during their stay in Maryland and had become very attached to little "Scottie," her five-year-old cousin. Her most vivid recollection of that visit, Marjorie told me, was the almost nightly appearance of the genial, bumbling giant, Tom Wolfe, with bottle in hand. After supper the two men would adjourn to their habitual deck chairs in the dark of the open terrace, talking the night away as the level in the two bottles sank lower and lower. Sometimes in the very early morning, Marjorie would look out of her window upstairs to see one or both of them still there, sound asleep.

Marjorie's house was full of pictures Zelda had painted, abstract oils as colorful and strange as her own personality. I liked some of them—one in particular of a white lily rising from blackness into a red mass that seemed to symbolize death to life—but most of them I couldn't understand. There were so many that Marjorie had to store the overflow in the garage where, sadly, they were later destroyed in a fire. Marjorie's daughter, Sayre, inherited the remaining paintings, but I have one which Marjorie gave me. It is of pastel-hued flowers in a lopsided vase which, like its ill-fated artist, seemed impossibly off balance. But my husband would not let me hang it because it made him nervous.

Occasionally Marjorie would show me letters which Zelda wrote her from the sanitorium, some of them beautifully phrased and some of them almost incoherent. When I heard that Zelda's condition had improved and that she was coming back to Montgomery, I looked forward to meeting her, but Marjorie told me she was still very nervous and preferred to see only her mother and a few close friends. Sometimes, though, I would see Zelda taking her long-striding, solitary walks, her hair unkempt, her thin figure in its old sweater bent into the wind, and I would wonder at the almost complete disappearance of the youthful gaiety and charm which former friends remembered so well.

One day I arrived at Marjorie's house to find her red-eyed from lack of sleep and furious at the behavior of some of Zelda's "so-called friends," as she expressed it, who were not proving too helpful in Zelda's long and losing battle against recurring mental illness. "They knew that she simply cannot drink," Marjorie raged, "yet they insist on inviting her to parties where they know liquor will be served. Zelda was always the center of all the fun when she was young, and they still expect her to be witty and sparkling. They can't seem to realize that those times are over and that she needs help!"

"Can't you explain the situation?" I ventured.

"They aren't interested in anyone but themselves," Marjorie complained. "Zelda was a big name for a while and it gives them some reflected glory to entertain for her. Then they say, 'Oh, a little sherry won't hurt you!' and one thing leads to another. It ends up that *we* get a phone call in the middle of the night and find her in such a state that we have to get a nurse and a hypodermic to calm her down! Some friends! They're doing everything possible to put Zelda back in the hospital."

Though there were backslidings like that on occasion, it did finally seem that Zelda was winning her battle, with the constant help of her wonderful mother. Mama Sayre encouraged her to take long walks and also to sew and cook—Zelda was expert at both—to add to her fine collection of classical records and, in the end, when everything else failed, she prayed with her, the two women kneeling by Zelda's bed as they had done when she was a small girl. Marjorie told me once that Zelda's knees were actually raw from her long hours of kneeling.

Finally there came the day when Marjorie told me Zelda felt much improved and would like to invite me to tea. We spent a pleasant hour with her in Mama Sayre's small cottage. Zelda was in good spirits, telling us how she had made the decorated cookies and showing recent snapshots of Scottie's children with obvious pleasure. Suddenly without warning she said quietly, "I hope you girls will excuse me if I rest now. I feel a little nervous." Without waiting for an answer she went into her bedroom and shut the door. I would not see her again. Within a few weeks, I learned that she had boarded the train alone for the sanitorium in North Carolina where she and many other mental patients were fated to die tragically when fire destroyed the building.

It was at the time of Zelda's little tea party that I first met Mama Sayre, as Marjorie called her. Robert Frost, at one of his last campus appearances, told the college gathering, "My greatest pleasure nowadays is in looking for kindred spirits." He would have found one in Mama Sayre if he could have met her, as I did, during her eighty-sixth year. There is even a physical resemblance, the same startlingly blue eyes framed by soft white hair, the healthy glow of the skin, the alive look of them both. Especially, though, they shared that rare quality of living completely in the moment, of giving absorbed attention to the persons present, and of gracing the most casual occasion with the almost forgotten art of wonderful storytelling.

The youthful charm and gaiety with which Zelda once captured the hearts of the "international set" must have come from her mother, for her father, an Alabama Supreme Court judge and author of many weighty legal tomes, was a severe and rather humorless disciplinarian. Zelda and her three older sisters and brother fully expected to be sent from the table without supper if they were late in arriving or unmannerly in conduct. Although Mama Sayre undoubtedly spoiled her adored youngest daughter, she nevertheless gave her a happy girlhood full of love.

I went to call on Mama Sayre a short time after hearing of Zelda's death. I was afraid I might find her crushed with grief, but tragedy was an old, familiar acquaintance of Mama Sayre's, one to whom she could say calmly, "I know you and I'm not afraid. There's nothing more you can do to me." The first great tragedy that shadowed her girlhood was the death of her three little sisters during the Civil War. Born Minerva Machen in Eddyville, Kentucky, on her father's big tobacco plantation, little Minnie, as she was called, was interned with her mother under harsh and primitive conditions in Canada while her father served in the Senate for the Confederacy. But after the long war years were over and Minnie grew to young womanhood, her golden ringlets and charm brought a flock of suitors to her door. I have seen a picture of her taken about this time. Across the corner some long-forgotten admirer had written, "To the Wild Lily of the Cumberland."

The early years of Minnie's marriage to Anthony Sayre, the young lawyer whom she finally chose, were happy ones.

In the white frame house on Court Street in Montgomery to which the young couple moved, two children were soon born. The first baby, a daughter, was fretful and sickly, but the son, his mother told me, was "the most healthy, beautiful boy I ever saw." Then tragedy struck again. "One day," Mama Sayre said, remembering, "my little boy was laughing and running around the house. The next day he was dead—of spinal meningitis. I wanted to die, too. I shut myself up in my room, refusing to see anyone or eat. I lay on the bed and turned my face to the wall. For a while they humored me and it might have gone on like that for no telling how long. Then something happened that changed my life. Our family doctor forced his way in. He was a wise old man and knew how to treat me. He took me by the shoulders and made me look at him. 'Minnie,' he said, 'I know how you feel. But you've got a lonely little girl downstairs who needs you. What's past is past. You've got to live for the living.'"

Mama Sayre repeated the words again with a small catch in her rich voice, "You must live for the living. I've remembered that all these years!"

We were sitting in the cheerful parlor of Mama Sayre's small frame house—the "Rabbit Run," her family called it because it was long and narrow—to which she had moved after Judge Sayre and her second son died, as the girls were all married. Everything in the room spoke of comfort and warmth—the open grate fire, the wide-armed rockers and chintz-covered sofa, the pictures and mementos on the mantel, the breakfront, and Zelda's old upright piano. There, too, was the familiar picture of Scott Fitzgerald's angelic profile.

But I heard Mama Sayre speak of him only once in the ten years I knew her, "He was a handsome thing; I'll say that for him. But he was not good for my daughter and he gave her things she shouldn't have. He was a selfish man. What he wanted always came first." It was not said bitterly, only sadly. Then she turned from the picture and spoke of other, pleasanter things.

More than likely there would be other visitors—people who enjoyed forgetting their troubles briefly in the pleasure of listening to Mama Sayre's anecdotes. The "regulars" were an oddly assorted group, for her interest in and curiosity about people were boundless. Judge Sayre used to call them "Minnie's Menagerie," for these afternoon visiting sessions had begun long before his death. "How were your crazy folks today, Mama?" he would ask indulgently as he came in from the office.

I was sadly reminded of Mama Sayre's callers just recently when I saw in the morning newspaper an account of the death from malnutrition of one of them, her gentle poet, an absentminded, harmless old recluse who lived in a veritable tunnel of musty books and papers. Mama Sayre gave him the food he needed most—she listened to his poems and to his philosophical ramblings about the meaning of life. His favorite overstuffed chair was always waiting, but whenever she saw him shuffling up the walk, someone had to run quickly and fetch doilies for the chair arms. "He's a very sweet man," she would say, "and I do like him, but his hands are so dirty!"

There was the spastic girl, intelligent and not unattractive, but painfully shy in company because of the awful contortions of her face. In that comfortable presence she became just like anybody else, as she put it, marveling. Not long ago I heard that she is happily married to a man who, like herself, is handicapped.

Another of the regular callers was a faded beauty who talked endlessly about her miraculous grandchildren and the long-past glamour of her family history. If Mama Sayre grew bored by those long recitals, she never showed it. Occasionally a name from the past would spark one of her delightful stories.

"Oh, yes, *that* governor!" she said once. "His wife came to call on me when my husband was first appointed judge. I was so frightened for fear everything wouldn't be just right—I'd heard she was a very particular person—so I had the house and the children scrubbed and shining way ahead of time. When I heard the knocker I sailed into the parlor in my best bib and tucker, swung the door open—and then," she chuckled, to punctuate the dramatic climax, "we looked down at the same instant and I was horrified! A row of chamber pots sat in a long line beside the front door, all full of great lumps of coal. Little Tony—he was about two then—had slipped away from me somehow and had collected them from under all the beds! But do you know," she ended, "that governor's wife was human after all. She threw back her head and nearly died laughing and that broke the ice. There was nothing for me to do but laugh, too, and we became great friends."

I never met the Mormon missionary, but I heard about him from Mama Sayre's oldest daughter, Marjorie's mother, who lived next door. "He thinks he's converting Mama to Mormonism," she laughed. "Why, Mama's always been a strict Episcopalian and always will be. But she's having the time of her life finding out all about the Mormons. She has that young fellow's tongue going a mile a minute answering her questions."

There was another young man whose mission was to find out about the history of Montgomery's old houses. Of this caller Mama Sayre said, "I can't imagine why he came to me and I told him so. 'Young man,' I said, 'I can't tell you much about *Montgomery's* houses. I came from Kentucky!'"

Strangely enough, she didn't seem to understand why I found this so funny. At the time she had been in Montgomery only seventy-five years.

Perhaps the years had gone quickly for her because her life was so full of friends who brought the world into her parlor. Her rheumatism, which must have been painful though she never spoke of it, made it increasingly difficult for her to get around. I think the last time she left her house was when she had someone drive her to the cemetery to the burial of Marjorie Noble, her favorite granddaughter and my dearest friend, who died of cancer. I know she missed Marjorie, who was so like her in temperament, but still there were always the living.

There were a few occasions when Zelda and Scott's daughter, "Scottie" Lanahan, and her husband flew down from New York or Washington with a nurse and one or another of their four children.

Scottie's husband, who had been raised in a luxurious mansion in the East, remarked that he had never known a spot more comfortable and pleasant than one of Mama Sayre's rocking chairs.

The morning routine rarely varied. On good days, Mama Sayre sat on the porch, a wide and genial figure among her potted plants and climbing roses. The postman, the Negro vegetable woman, always stopped for a chat, their faces brightening as they neared the house. It was in an old-fashioned neighborhood, growing a little down-at-the-heels, but there were the same kindly neighbors and the familiar tree-shaded sidewalk where something was always happening. Changes were almost imperceptible, but once I remember she shook her head sadly at the noisy brood of children who had moved in across the street. "Bottom rail's settin' on top," she murmured. "Children nowadays don't know their manners!"

Such critical comments from her were rare. Her usual calm acceptance of each day's events reflected an inner poise. Somewhere recently I came across the expression "inner-directed," which perhaps describes it best. I am reminded, too, of John Burrough's description of the aging Whitman—"slow of movement, tolerant, receptive, democratic, and full of charity and good will towards all—a life contentedly and joyously lived."

The end came quietly in her ninety-sixth year. I went to the hospital where they had taken her. "The doctor gave us a choice," her daughter told me. "He might prolong her life a few months by an operation, but I don't think Mama would want it that way. He's promised us he won't let her be in pain. But please talk to her. She does love visitors so—and I don't like to leave her alone."

A pretty nurse greeted me at the door of the room. I'm so glad you've come," she told me. "She loves people to talk to her. She's got me telling her all about my boy friend and where I come from . . ." Mama Sayre was just waking from a doze but the blue eyes shone with instant recognition and the smile and lovely voice were unchanged.

"Come sit here and hold my hand," she beckoned me, "and tell me all about yourself." I kissed her when I left and pressed the soft cheek. I, too, hated to leave her alone, but I had work to do at home. Next day, I heard she had died in her sleep.

Last year the little house we called the "Rabbit Run" was torn down to make way for the new interstate highway, but it lives vividly in my mind. In these heedless days when our gentle old people are so often put aside into nursing homes, I think with love and gratitude of the sunlit afternoons in that little parlor and Mama Sayre telling stories.

Chapter Sixteen

"Aunt Mary"

It was late in the Depression summer of 1936. My young husband and I had sold our furniture in anticipation of a proffered job that had fallen through and now, with a baby only six weeks old, we were flat broke. In that dilemma, it was natural for us to remember my family's cabin, Dogwood Lodge, where we had spent a brief April honeymoon two years before. My parents, in the midst of their annual move back to town, were obliging but dubious. With middle-aged practicality, the pair reminded us that there was no electricity, that the log fire did not begin to heat the vast living room in winter, that we would be on a winding dirt road fourteen lonely miles from town.

Our argument was unanswerable—the lodge was free and we had literally nowhere else to go—unless we lived with my parents which, in our youthful independence, we refused to consider. At least we would have running water—Daddy had built a rock reservoir around a spring on a higher hill—and for neighbors there would be the elderly Negro couple in the caretakers' cabin. Ed, with his wagon and mules, would keep us supplied with logs from the surrounding acres, and we savoured the thought of Evie's fresh eggs and her fabulous butter.

Thus began a memorable three months. A job in a service station materialized at the last possible moment—twelve hours a day at sixty dollars a month. We figured that with careful budgeting we could manage, although just barely. We set aside twenty dollars for gasoline, thirty for food, and ten for extras. I recall, for example, a frantic ride over that mountain road to the doctor's house the night the baby had a fever. There was no telephone, of course. Also, my poor husband had little chance to enjoy the beautiful woods. It was still dark when he left the lodge at five in the morning and it was dark when he returned at seven. I contrived a blanket sling in which I carried the baby on my back Indian-style, so I could go for walks along the winding creek banks or on the ridges of the hills. It was on one of those walks that I discovered Aunt Mary.

I had known for some time that there were hill people on the far side of the woods because one family often took a short cut down our trail on their way to church. They walked single file, the man in front in his white Sunday shirt, the wife following, then the children in order of size. I waved to the small ones, but they only glanced at me like frightened deer as they scurried to keep up with their father's long strides. Aunt Mary was shy at first, too, but my baby's smile won her over.

Aunt Mary's house was on the near side of the woods across the railroad, an unpainted, shingle-roofed cabin perched on a high bank. I was first attracted by the profusion of bright flowers bordering the dirt walk and the comfortable porch. Then I fell under the spell of Aunt Mary herself. She was a tall, angular woman with stringy hair in a tight bun and an ankle-length cotton print dress—almost a caricature of a Grant Wood painting. Her thin, lined face lit up with a beautiful smile when I admired her flowers, and she recounted their histories—the ones found in the woods and the ones raised from cuttings or from saving the seeds. Her harsh, nasal voice was almost gentle as she advised me about how to avoid "thrash" in the baby, and her gray eyes shone gratefully when I let her hold my little girl. When I asked her if she had any children, such a look of sadness came over her expressive face that I wished I'd never asked.

"Nary a one," she mourned. "I reckon the good Lord jest thought I warn't fitten fer to have none. I've jest got my Frank, praise be! We been married nigh onto fifty year." She did have nephews, however, who had started everybody calling her "Aunt Mary." As I prepared to depart for home, Aunt Mary told me more about Frank, apologizing for his not coming out of the house to greet me. "He don't see people much any more on account of his face; the doctor cain't seem to cure it up. But Frank takes good keer of me, even if he cain't work like he use ter."

Frank had never had a chance to get "book-larnin'," Aunt Mary said, but he could "make change as good as a banker, and nobody ever cheated him out of a cent. And *smart?*" She told me proudly how Frank could sit right there while a string of fifty freight cars passed, and he could name off every single one of those long numbers painted on the sides of the cars. None of this quite prepared me for meeting Frank, a mild little man who finally came shyly onto the porch as I was leaving. He had a red cotton bandanna tied slantwise across one cheek, but a gust of wind blew the scarf briefly aside. My polite smile felt suddenly frozen. The whole side of his face was eaten away by cancer.

Aunt Mary tactfully covered my dismay by suggesting that perhaps I would like to buy some of her eggs each week. With relief, we turned to bargaining, as the sick feeling in my stomach gradually eased. Thereafter, I grew to look forward to Aunt Mary's weekly visits, particularly when I discovered that she had an unexpectedly wry, sarcastic wit. Once she remarked that she had to get along a little slower now than she used to, "but that's the way a lawyer gits to heaven, I reckon, by degrees!"

It amazed me to learn that Aunt Mary, like her husband, was completely illiterate. "There warn't no schools when I was a little 'un," she explained. "When the Yankees come through here, they took our crops and they took our animals. Right here where we stand was our corn field!" She spread out her long arms and stood silent, looking up at the great pines towering above us, seeing it again and making me see it, too. "The first game I remember playing was my sister and me taking turns at being the mule. I'd hitch her to the plow, and then she'd hitch me to the plow, small as I was. It still makes me feel tired to think on it!" She looked down at her knotted hands and sighed, "Ah, well, that was long ago. The young 'uns now, they has it better than us." She turned the talk to her nephew's good schooling, of his fine house in town and his good job at the iron foundry.

It was not long after this talk that the cold weather set in, and my parents' predictions came true. We were cold! We suspended blankets from the balcony at night to make a tent around the great stone fireplace. We tried everything, but it was no use. Finally, although the baby stayed rosy with health, my husband and I both got influenza and regretfully we conceded defeat. I found that I could earn the munificent sum of three dollars a day as a substitute in the county schools. With this windfall we could salve our pride by paying twenty dollars a month to my family for board. I promised Aunt Mary I would come often to see her, but I grew busy with my new life in town and the months slipped away. It was almost summer before we began going back for weekends at the log cabin.

One summer day, as I sat on the porch watching the baby practicing her first steps, I saw Aunt Mary's familiar, awkward figure coming up the woods path. She was delighted with the baby's antics and, for a few minutes, it seemed like old times. Then unaccountably she grew silent, staring off into the pines as she had when she had told me about the Yankees. Suddenly her long face crumpled like that of a child, and she covered it with her bony hands. "I see you don't know, and I've got to say it. I jes cain't find the words." Her shoulders trembled once in a soundless sob. Then she took down her hands and said quietly, without expression, "Frank's gone. He got so finally—he—he starved to death!"

Then the tears came and I put my arms around her bent shoulders. In a little while, the spell of grief had passed and we talked of her plans. The nephews had been trying to persuade her to move to town but she didn't want to. She smiled at my toddler and held out her long arms.

"I didn't know you'd be here today," she said finally over the baby's curly head. "I jes come over to see this place agin. You know, I never bin out of sight of woods since I was born. I cain't seem to set my mind on goin' to town . . ."

I never saw Aunt Mary again.

Chapter Seventeen

Rebel to the End

Even at Daddy's funeral Mother remained a rebel. She shocked the conventional friends who visited the house by receiving them in a flaming red dress because, she said, that had been Daddy's favorite color. Instead of a period of mourning and of placing funeral wreaths in the cemetery, Mother insisted that she stay alone at Dogwood Lodge, where she and Daddy had spent so many happy years. I think the spot she liked best of all was the small private porch Ed had built for her outside her upstairs bedroom overlooking the pool. It became her custom to sit there every evening in the darkness, sipping her drink and watching the creek as it reflected the outside lights strung among the trees.

Though Mother continued her golf games and the weekly Bingo nights at the country club, often she must have been miserably lonely, for the lodge was too far from town for visits from her friends. By this time, too, merry Nell Clarkson and lovely Jean Moody were dead, and many of her other old friends had problems of their own. Sarah Moody was nursing an invalid husband; Ira Moody, now widowed, had taken a job; and the Strodes spent much of their time in foreign travel. As none of the family lived in Tuscaloosa then, we could only worry and argue while Mother turned a deaf ear, although she did finally consent to installing an electric buzzer that connected with Ed's cabin on the hill.

I suspected that Mother often drank more than she should during those days, and a strange, rather mysterious incident made me certain. One night Ed was awakened by the sound of gunshots and came running down the hill to find Mother with a smoking revolver in her hand. She had shot out every pane in her bedroom window. Eventually she made Ed go back to bed, insisting that she was perfectly safe. What it was she saw—or thought she saw—we were never able to find out.

Certainly, by nature, Mother was never one to brood, and if she had her bad moments, she kept them to herself. She went alone on the Caribbean cruise she and Daddy had planned before his death. She drove to Houston, Texas, to help my sister Virginia locate a new house, and she traveled to Europe to visit my younger sister Peggy whose officer husband was then stationed in Germany. Shortly before that last journey, Mother had lost her big toe. The doctor was forced to amputate it as the result of a cancerous mole. Perhaps that event should have warned us—but Mother joked about the lost digit and insisted that it didn't prevent her from having the most glorious trip since her honeymoon.

I had almost forgotten the lost toe when the ominous long distance call came two years later. It was Dr. Shamblin—old Dr. Max had by then retired—calling from the hospital in defiance of Mother's orders. The melanoma cancer had recurred and had reached her knee and minutes were important. However, Mother flatly refused to lose her leg or even to notify us. "I've managed to get her in the hospital for a checkup," Dr. Shamblin told us, "though she swore when I amputated her toe that I'd never get her back here again. But if you can't get over here and talk some sense into her before eight o'clock tomorrow morning, she'll walk out of here and be dead in six months!"

The scene in Mother's hospital room the next day was both pathetic and funny. Like a sulky child she propped her newspaper in front of her face and pretended to ignore us. Each time I mentioned her leg, she changed the subject. Finally, I grabbed the paper and held it down while I pleaded with her, but I made no headway until I reminded her that I was talking for my brother and my sisters who were too far away to come. We had always admired Mother's courage—she had proved it by living alone at the lodge. What would the others think of her now? Finally, reluctantly, she gave her consent, and the operation was performed within the hour.

I must sadly report that Mother was not the least bit grateful for our interference, as she called it, nor was she a model patient. She was furious with Dr. Shamblin, or pretended to be, although I think that kind man understood her need to shout her anger at a fate she could not accept. She was as fiercely independent as ever, and the nurses had to restrain her from trying to hop across the room to the bathroom on one leg. When we showed her newspaper clippings about one-legged people who played golf or flew airplanes, she would point out unanswerably, "But he's young and he has a knee! Look at all that Dr. Shamblin's left for me!" And she'd jerk up her skirt and poke the stump of her leg at us, no matter who was present.

One good result of Mother's complete frankness and lack of embarrassment about the missing limb was that it was impossible for people to be ill at ease in her presence. After we took her home, there was a constant stream of visitors, even some of her old friends whom she had somewhat neglected in recent years. "They know I'll come to see them when it's raining and I can't play golf," she used to say. I think Mother was touched by her friends' loyalty now, but the tribute that really moved her most deeply was the flowers from her three favorite golfing friends with a miniature loving cup inscribed "To our first lady of golf." Mother posed proudly in her wheelchair for a news story under the same heading which stated that her record of nine holes in thirty-five strokes playing from men's tees in tournament play had not yet been equaled by a local woman. Members of the ladies' golf group which Mother had organized to play and lunch together on Fridays announced plans to donate a silver loving cup in honor of Mother each year to the member who made the most improvement in her game.

We hoped Mother's artificial leg would arrive, and that she would learn to use it in time for her to award that trophy in person at the finale of the local tournament. She flatly refused to go in her wheelchair. Meanwhile, after a long and frustrating search for a nurse who would live in the house and prepare simple meals, we found Mrs. Allen. She was as expert a nurse as her admirers claimed and was glad to be living near her husband, who was a mental patient at the Veterans Hospital—but Lord, she was ugly! An awkward, gangling woman with a knot of stringy hair, Mrs. Allen was surprisingly gentle with her refractory patient and also an excellent cook. Unfortunately Mother, with her love of beauty, developed an aversion to the poor woman which she made no effort to overcome. I think it was mainly because of the teeth! Mrs. Allen's false teeth were apparently uncomfortable and she would remove them in the evenings while she regaled Mother with interminable conversations which Mother, then grown quite deaf, could not begin to understand. "I wouldn't mind so much if she'd just keep quiet and let me read my book," Mother would complain when we paid our weekend visits. "But I've fixed her now! I've moved the big table lamp between us and turned my chair sideways, so I don't have to look at her!"

At least our nurse accomplished one good purpose—she fired Mother with the eagerness to learn to use the new leg so that she would get rid of Mrs. Allen. It was not an easy chore for a woman nearly seventy, strong and active as Mother had always been, and the task was further complicated by Mother's fear of falling. In time, however, she learned to walk around the house and finally the day came when she drove proudly away in her shabby Oldsmobile. She watched the finish of the golf matches from her car, shopped from the curb at the grocery and the liquor store, and even hazarded one trip to Dogwood Lodge. Although she steadily refused to leave the driver's seat, not daring to trust the cumbersome, hated prosthesis, we hoped that before long she would begin to be her old, active self again, but that was not to be. After one unlucky excursion, the heavy leg slipped off as she was getting out of the car, leaving her sitting helplessly in the backyard for hours. She never drove again.

On the whole, however, those first five years in the wheelchair had their compensations. There were the wonderful long visits from her old friend Mary Bacon from her home in Daphne on Mobile Bay. Mary Bacon was a stimulating companion despite her years of crippling arthritis. Mother's former golfing mate, Lista Eddins, never failed to come on Sundays after church. Hudson and Theresa Strode never neglected her, and Sarah Moody often came for good talk of books and world affairs. Mother also kept a big scrapbook of interesting items from the papers and magazines.

She spent most of each day surrounded by stacks of new books in the comfortable reclining chair which the four of us had given her at Christmas and which she'd placed in a sunny corner overlooking the back garden. She watered her azaleas from the porch, fed seeds to the song birds, and directed the colored yard man, Reuben, who came twice a week, trying to find an unoccupied spot for the new plants she ordered from the ever-present flower catalogues, The university boys in the upstairs apartments took a proprietary interest in Mother, too. She was much too indulgent with the students, and they sometimes took advantage of her.

However, we blessed their presence then, for without them, we would never have dared to accede to Mother's determination to live alone. Mrs. Allen's departure had been hastened by Mother's belated discovery that the nurse had secretly been dipping into her precious liquor supply and filling up the bottles with coffee!

During those years Mother was very careful to control her drinking, primarily because of her determination not to fall, a resolution underscored by the death of two of her friends from that cause. At night, however, she would occasionally drink after she was ensconced in bed in the one-time dining—room for the ritual evening television, "I've got you now!" Mother would scream at the suave announcer of the Alka Seltzer commercial as she cut him off in mid-spiel with her treasured remote control gadget. "I guess that'll teach you not to say 'stummick'!" It was something of an ordeal for any of us to watch TV with her, as her growing deafness made her increase the volume past any hope of conversation. I must admit that we were relieved when a gentle snore from the propped up pillows would allow us to turn down the volume.

The beginning of Mother's decline was so gradual that at first we didn't notice it. There was a slow accumulation of small disappointments. As her friendly students graduated, they were replaced by a strange long-haired group who moved out the furniture and put mattresses and candles on the floor. Then Reuben quit his job to go on welfare. The old man wasn't good for much and always smelled of whiskey, but Mother had grown to depend on him. Fewer callers came in the afternoons as Mother's deafness made conversation difficult, and she adamantly refused a hearing aid. The ancient rusty water pipes burst while her students were away on vacation, flooding out the gas furnace and leaving her shivering helplessly until our arrival days later. Then Katherine died. She was the devoted beauty parlor operator who had come to the house every Monday to fix Mother's hair. Katherine proved to be irreplaceable. Looking back, however, I believe the severest blow to Mother was the loss of her teeth.

Up to that time, Mother had never had a tooth filled, and the roots were still perfect but since her confinement, she had fallen into a careless diet of too many sweets and soft foods. As a result, her teeth began to break off until there were almost none left and we had no recourse except to have the rotten stubs pulled. Mother never tried seriously to eat with the hated false teeth and used them as an excuse practically to stop eating altogether. Family and friends pleaded to no avail. Her sisters, all wonderful cooks, vainly tempted her with baskets of delicious foods on their frequent visits from Birmingham. Mother would not or could not—eat.

We began to suspect, too, that she had stopped using the artificial leg. Her protestations to the contrary had a false ring and she was never a good liar. One day, she finally admitted that the limb did not seem to fit right any more and supposed she must have lost some weight. We pretended to be appeased by her promises to do better, but soon we became aware of an even more alarming fact. It was her good friend Sarah Moody who first noticed it—Mother had stopped reading.

"She has that same book open every time I come," Sarah pointed out, "but I don't believe she's turned a page in two weeks."

I think we gave up hope then. Mother had said so often that she could bear anything as long as she had her books. Of two friends in the neighborhood who became mentally ill, Mother had commented, "Well, I guess I'm lucky after all; I'd rather lose a leg than my mind." We had tried to pretend that Mother's repetitions were the result of drinking. Now we knew the cause was something more.

The crisis came on Homecoming Day, the big day of the year in Tuscaloosa, when everyone closes shop to watch the parade and the game, and every street is choked with cars of returning grads and party-goers. Mother had ordered tickets for us a year in advance and we were to meet my brother and his wife Edith at the house. At first things seemed normal, Mother in her chair among the books and wearing her gay red dress in honor of the occasion. Then all of us began to be aware of a strained brightness in her chatter and a strange rigidity of posture, almost as though she were forcing herself to sit upright. Something was wrong!

Then I noticed the frightened face of the colored maid, Jesselia, when she beckoned me silently into the bedroom. "Miss Helen, yo' mama didn' want me to tell you, but she bin real sick. We is all out of clean sheets."

I gasped. "Why, Jesselia, we can't be! I just bought half a dozen—I knew we'd be having company . . ."

"Jes look," Jesselia interrupted me with a gesture toward a great mound of soiled bedclothes. "Ev'y day when I come, she in the bed sick. I wanted to phone like you say, but she beg me so . . ."

"Maybe she's feeling better today," I ventured doubtfully. "She doesn't look so bad."

Jesselia shook her head sadly. "It took her mos' an hour to git fum the bed to the chair. I never see anything so pitiful." She began to cry. "She kep' sayin' over and over, 'Don't help me; I kin do it mysef . . .' but she couldn', Miss Helen, she jes' couldn'."

Yet somehow Mother had! For there she sat in her red dress and her false gaiety telling us to hurry—we mustn't miss the kickoff and she'd be listening on the radio. When Edith slipped away to join me in the kitchen, we assessed the problem of getting Mother to the hospital. At that hour of Homecoming Day, the feat could only have been managed by helicopter and all of the doctors would be watching the game. Finally, we sent the men off to the stadium with whispered explanations that we would follow later. Then we tried vainly for another hour to get Mother out of her chair and back to bed. She refused to budge and we couldn't lift her.

In the end, to please Mother, Edith and I had to go to the game.

After the game, as soon as the traffic cleared and we could contact the doctor and the hospital, my brother picked up Mother and carried her to the car fighting all the way, kicking and screaming, "I'm not going to the hospital. You can't make me! I want to stay in my beautiful house!"

Mother would have two months in the hospital before her death. Eventually she adjusted to the inevitable—she had more resilience than we gave her credit for—and most of the time she was lucid. Sometimes, however, waking from a doze, Mother would think she was back in her Pinehurst home. Pointing to the closet door, she would call out to a bewildered nurse, "Honey, run back to the kitchen and get yourself something to eat . . . The icebox is just full of things my sisters brought. Just help yourself!"

After the loneliness of the last few years, she enjoyed being the center of attention again—the renewed visits from her faithful friends, a Thanksgiving visit from Virginia and her family from Texas. Mother seemed almost her old self when Peggy arrived from Korea—flown home by the Army because Mother's illness was terminal. Peggy even persuaded Mother to eat a few meals and decorated her room with colorful Christmas cards and a little silver tree. At last, however, everyone had to leave. I had insisted that my husband go home, too, to spend Christmas Day with our teenage daughter and his elderly mother—so I was alone with Mother when she died in her sleep. It was nearly midnight on Christmas Eve.

The impersonal efficiency of a great modern hospital robs grief of its poignancy. It was not until I was in the taxi surrounded by the miscellaneous clutter of Mother's flowers and boxes that I began to feel the loneliness of the empty streets—a loneliness accentuated by the occasional glow of a Christmas tree over which parents were laboring to surprise their children. The taxi driver was a kind-looking elderly gentleman, and I wasn't surprised to learn that he was the owner of the cab company who had let off his men for the holiday.

After he had turned on the lights for me in Mother's empty house and placed the boxes inside, and after I was somewhat comforted by a phone call to my husband, I could no longer put off notifying the family.

First, however, I opened the suitcase I had brought from the hospital and placed the contents in their old places around the empty chair—Mother's treasured photographs of Daddy, the four of us, the twelve grandchildren and the five great-grandchildren; the yellowed clippings of her golf triumphs; her latest book—it was *The Source* by Michener—with the bookmark still in the same place. I remembered how she had looked as she sat in that chair, rigid with pain, urging us to hurry to the football game. She wouldn't want to spoil anyone's Christmas morning. A few more hours would not matter.

Only Mother would ever have thought that shabby old house beautiful. Within months, a wealthy neighbor purchased it and had it torn down to make a space for a garden. There would be only a caretaker at Dogwood Lodge which we kept with its surrounding woods, although it gets increasingly difficult to get our scattered family together. Mother had been the force uniting us through all those summers. The log walls of the lodge are full of reminders—dozens of her books in the big bookcases, the rock walls and benches, the thrift and iris she set out on the terraces over the pool. Perhaps in our growing jungle of asphalt and noise, we'll find a way to keep alive for our children that one unspoiled place that Mother loved.

As I sat by her chair in the empty house on that lonely Christmas Eve, I suddenly realized that the frail figure in the hospital bed was not the Mother I would remember. Mother was very much alive—contradictory and courageous, selfish and generous, exuberant and timid, tactless and kind—in a word, indestructible, a rebel to the end!

www.ingramcontent.com/pod-product-compliance
Lightning Source LLC
Chambersburg PA
CBHW022100160426
43198CB00008B/300